RAISING GIRLS
IN TODAY'S DIGITAL WORLD

Positive Parenting Tips for Raising Strong Girls,
and Confident Creative Daughters

Bukky Ekine-Ogunlana

© Copyright Bukky Ekine-Ogunlana 2025 – All rights reserved.

The content of this book may not be reproduced, duplicated, or transmitted without direct written permission from the author or the publisher.

Under no circumstance will any blame or legal responsibility be held against the publisher, or author, for any damages, reparation, or monetary loss due to the information contained within this book. Either directly or indirectly. You are responsible for your own choices, actions, and results.

Legal Notice:

This book is copyright protected. This book is only for personal use. You cannot amend, distribute, sell, use, quote, or paraphrase any part, or the content within this book, without the consent of the author or publisher.

Disclaimer Notice:

Please note the information contained within this document is for educational and entertainment purposes only. All effort has been executed to present accurate, up-to-date, and reliable, complete information. No warranties of any kind are declared or implied. Readers acknowledge that the author is not engaging in the rendering of legal, financial, medical, or professional advice. The content within this book has been derived from various sources. Please consult a licensed professional before attempting any techniques outlined in this book

By reading this document, the reader agrees that under no circumstances is the author responsible for any losses, direct or indirect, which are incurred as a result of the use of the information contained within this document, including, but not limited to,—errors, omissions, or inaccuracies.

Published by

TCEC Publishing

TCEC House. UK

Dedication

This book is dedicated to our three amazing children and all the beautiful children worldwide who have passed through the T.C.E.C 6-16 years program over the years. Thank you for the opportunity to serve you and invest in your colorful and bright future.

Table of Content

Introduction *Raising Girls with Courage, Calm, and Character in a Loud, Pressured World* 7

Chapter 1: *Laying Foundations The Discovery Years (Birth to Age 5)* .. 13

Chapter 2 *The Early Years (Ages 5–7)* 24

Chapter 3 *Developmental Milestones (Ages 6–10)* 36

Chapter 4: *Cultivating Creativity (Ages 7–10)* 46

Chapter 5: *Building Strong Relationships with Your Daughter* 56

Chapter 6: *Ambition and Education* 67

Chapter 7: *The Internet and Media* 77

Chapter 8: *The Joy of Raising Daughters* 89

Chapter 9: *Body Image, Puberty & Identity* 99

Chapter 10: *Friendships, Boundaries & Consent Growing Connection, Confidence & Courage* 112

Chapter 11: *Financial Independence & Purpose Raising Girls Who Know Their Worth And How to Manage It* 125

Chapter 12: *Mental Health & Emotional Resilience* 136

Chapter 13: *Raising Girls of Heritage / Cultural Identity* 142

Please leave a 1-click Review! 153

Conclusion *The Journey of Raising a Girl With Purpose* 154

Other Books You'll Love! 158

References 162

Introduction
Raising Girls with Courage, Calm, and Character in a Loud, Pressured World

There's something tender, complex, and deeply rewarding about raising a daughter. Whether you've just brought her home from the hospital or you're navigating the tears, eye-rolls, or silences of a teenage girl—you're not alone. Raising a daughter today is no small task. It's a beautiful journey—but it can also feel confusing, exhausting, even scary.

We've all asked ourselves questions like:

- *"Am I doing this right?"*
- *"Why does she cry so much over one comment?"*
- *"Why won't she talk to me anymore?"*
- *"How can I protect her without making her afraid of the world?"*

This book is here to walk with you through all of that—like a trusted friend, an experienced mentor, and a flashlight on a foggy path.

Why This Book?

Let's be honest—there are already so many great books out there. So why add another one? Because this one's different. It brings together biblical truth, real psychological insight, and everyday conversations in a way that's practical and down-to-earth.

You'll find tools you can actually use—right away. We'll give you real words for the tough moments and share stories of both wins and missteps from real families (mine included).

We'll talk honestly about the hard stuff—comparison, body image, fear, loneliness, broken friendships, and choices we wish we could take back. And through it all, we'll look at the part God plays in your journey... and the part you do too.

This isn't about judgment. It's about walking through life together.

What You'll Find Inside

Each chapter focuses on a key area of your daughter's growth—confidence, identity, emotional safety, faith, courage, relationships, resilience. The book is built on three core beliefs:

1. **Girls are born with unique strength and sensitivity—both are gifts that need nurturing.**

2. **God's design for your daughter is not fear, but love, power, and a sound mind.**

3. **You, as her parent, are divinely positioned to be her safe place and guide.**

You'll find guidance tailored to different developmental stages—from age 3 to 12 and beyond—showing what's normal at 5 versus 15, and how to adjust your approach accordingly. Every chapter includes:

- *Milestone Moments* to help you recognize key phases.
- *Sample Scripts* to support honest conversations.
- *Real-life stories*—both joyful and painful—from parents who have walked this road.

For example:

Rachel, a single mom, helped her anxious 8-year-old name the worry voice in her head "Scared Sally." Together, they learned to speak truth louder than fear.

Contrast that with Isaac, who told his daughter to "toughen up" when she wanted to cry—without realizing he was shutting down her heart, making her stop coming to him with the big things.

This book is full of moments like these—not to make you feel guilty, but to show you what works and what doesn't. Reflection questions and action points close each chapter, so even busy parents can find practical takeaways. You can dive deep or jump straight to the *Parent Moves* sections for quick guidance.

A Word to Moms and Dads

Whether you're a single parent, a married couple, a blended family, or a guardian—you matter deeply in this journey.

- **Moms:** Your daughter often sees herself through your mirror. How you speak about your body, your emotions, and your past helps shape her identity.

- **Dads:** Your voice carries weight in ways you might not realize. Girls who hear love and approval from their fathers are more likely to thrive emotionally and spiritually—even in today's noisy world.

Your role doesn't need to be perfect. It needs to be *present*.

From the Bible—and From Today

Throughout this book, we'll draw some wisdom from Scripture—not as a rulebook, but as a source of deep encouragement. You'll meet:

- Esther, who was faced with fear but she found purpose.

- Miriam, who led with strength and humility.

- Mary, the young woman who carried the impossible and said "yes."

You'll also meet girls like:

- Jayla, a 14-year-old learning to navigate social media with support.

- Tara, a 6-year-old working through sensory challenges.

- Maya, a college-bound young woman wrestling with independence and faith.

Let's Be Honest
Parenting a girl today means you're probably navigating:

- Emotional ups and downs—sometimes within minutes.
- "Am I enough?" questions, even from little ones.
- Battles over screen time and the pull of social media influencers.
- Comparing your daughter's journey to others.
- Wondering if she's too shy, too loud, too sensitive—or just *right*.

This book helps replace fear with strategy, frustration with understanding, and doubt with confidence. It won't give you a script for every situation, but it *will* give you a way forward.

You Don't Have to Be Perfect—Just Present
You don't have to get it all right. You just have to show up, stay curious, and keep loving her—even when it's hard. Your daughter doesn't need a perfect parent. She needs *you*: showing up, apologizing when you mess up, speaking truth over her every day.

If you can do that, you're already doing better than you think.

A Note on Developmental Years (3—12)
This book focuses especially on the foundational years from early childhood through pre-adolescence. These years are full of discovery, growth, and identity-building. The way you

support her now lays the groundwork for the confident, resilient teen and adult she will become.

For Those Who Want to Go Deeper

If you want more nuanced strategies and insights for the teen years and beyond, I will like to invite you to explore my companion books:

- *Parenting Teen Girls*
- *Parenting Teenage Girls for Purpose*

Together, these resources provide a rich, ongoing roadmap to raise daughters with purpose, courage, and much joy.

Let's begin this journey—one brave, beautiful, imperfect, sacred step at a time.

After reading this guide, please feel free to leave a review based on your findings and how valuable the guide was to you. I would be incredibly thankful if you could take 60 seconds to write a brief review on the platform of purchase, even if it's just a few sentences!

Chapter 1
Laying Foundations
The Discovery Years (Birth to Age 5)

How Do I Raise My Daughter to Be Whole?

That's the quiet question many parents ask in the stillness after bedtime—when toys are tucked away, and the house is finally quiet. Raising a daughter isn't just about helping her grow up "good" or "successful." It's about raising a girl who knows she's *enough*—secure in her identity, full of courage, kindness, and resilience, and deeply aware of God's love for her.

But how do you do that in a world that starts shaping her ideas about herself before she even speaks full sentences?

The answer: start early. These first five years are more than cute giggles and scraped knees. They're the roots from which her entire sense of self will grow.

The First Five Years: More Than Just Toddler Time

We call them "toddler years," but really, these are the foundation years. Psychologists call this the attachment and discovery stage—when your daughter is asking, "Am I safe? Am I loved? Am I heard?" Scripture calls it "training her in the way she should go" (Proverbs 22:6). These early moments shape everything that comes after.

What She's Learning

From birth to age 5, your daughter will:

- **Build trust through your voice and touch.** Even as a baby, she knows when you're near and feels secure in your care.

- **Begin to explore her world with curiosity.** Her first words, her first steps, her first playtime adventures—all teaching her, "I am capable."

- **Start to understand emotions and relationships.** She learns what feelings are okay and how to express them.

- **Form early ideas about herself and others.** She hears messages about what girls "should" be like—messages that either limit or empower her.

- **Begin to grasp simple spiritual truths.** Even toddlers can understand love, kindness, and God's presence.

Developmental Milestones at a Glance (Ages 3–5)

Social & Emotional
- Plays well with other children
- Names emotions like happy, sad, mad, scared
- Shows empathy, like comforting a crying friend

Language & Communication
- Uses sentences of 4 to 6 words
- Asks lots of "why" questions (sometimes 50 in a row!)
- Follows two-step directions

Cognitive
- Understands concepts like "same vs different"
- Counts up to 10
- Sorts shapes and begins sequencing

Physical
- Climbs, hops, and skips
- Dresses with some help
- Draws simple shapes and stick figures

Remember, every child is unique. Some will reach milestones earlier or later, and that's okay. What matters most is that she feels safe and loved as she grows.

Planting Mental Health Seeds Early

Help her name her feelings: "Are you feeling angry or sad right now? It's okay to feel that way." This simple emotional coaching builds the foundation for resilience and healthy self-regulation later.

Teach her that her body belongs to her. She can say "no" to hugs or kisses if she's uncomfortable—even from family members. You can say, "You are the boss of your own body." These early lessons build trust in her instincts and boundaries.

Real life Story : Harry and Naomi

Harry and Florence's daughter Naomi was a shy 4-year-old. When Naomi got upset at school, Harry wanted to "toughen her up" for the world ahead. But Florence reminded him of Jesus' way—love first, strength grows from safety.

They began praying over Naomi, celebrating small acts of courage. Slowly, Naomi bloomed—not because she got louder or tougher, but because she felt seen, safe, and loved.

Scripture to Hold On To

Just like baby Moses was hidden and protected in the basket (Exodus 2), your daughter needs that same loving protection and prayers over her little life. Proverbs 22:6 reminds us: *"Train up a child in the way she should go; even when she is old she will not depart from it."*

Practical Parenting Moves for Ages 3–5

- **Name feelings out loud:** "You seem frustrated because your tower fell. That's okay."

- **Say simple prayers together:** "Thank you, God, for making you so special."

- **Model asking for forgiveness:** "I'm sorry I raised my voice. I love you."

- **Affirm character over appearance:** "I'm proud of how kind you were to your friend today."

- **Talk about body safety:** "You don't have to hug if you don't want to."

- **Question media together:** "Do you think that girl in the show is being kind?"

A Father's Blessing
Dads, your words carry power. Tell her:
- "I'm proud of you."
- "You don't have to be perfect—just be yourself."
- "You are brave, and I see it."
- "God is always with you, and so am I."

Final Thought: What You Sow Now Will Grow Later
The hours you spend reading stories, whispering prayers, and gently guiding her through big feelings are never wasted. These moments are *eternal deposits* into her heart.

You don't have to be perfect. You just have to be present.

Let's walk this beautiful, messy, sacred journey together—one tender step at a time.

How One Family Did It #1: Raising Naomi, Ages 0—5
A True Story of Real Parenting in the Early Years.

Florence sat on the edge of the bed, her newborn daughter sleeping against her chest, warm and tiny. The night lamp cast a soft glow over the nursery, and outside, rain tapped gently on the windowsill.

"I don't know if I'm doing this right," she whispered, her voice barely above a breath.

Harry was standing nearby, bottle in his hand, his eyes bleary from another sleepless night. He looked over at Florence and smiled wearily.

"Same," he said. "But she's here. And we're here. So maybe that's enough?"

They were new parents to Naomi—a very quiet, wide-eyed baby with a curious gaze and a gentle spirit. No one had prepared them for how disorienting the early months would be. But they'd made a decision, somewhere between the doctor's discharge instructions and their first diaper disaster:

We're not aiming for perfect. We're aiming to be present. And to do this with grace.

Trust Begins in the Smallest Moments

Every night, Harry took the late shift. He would pace the hallway with Naomi in his arms, whispering softly, "God made you, and I've got you." It became a kind of ritual. At first, he said it more for himself than for her.

But over time, those words became sacred—something he believed as much as he said.

Florence had her own rhythm. Each morning, before the house fully woke, she'd read Naomi *Goodnight Moon* and then speak a Psalm over her tiny daughter.

"She doesn't understand the words," Harry once said, watching them.

"She doesn't have to," Florence replied. "Her spirit hears."

They didn't follow a detailed parenting method. They just leaned into love, consistency, and presence. And slowly, they saw Naomi respond—with calm eyes, reaching hands, and a sense of safety that bloomed quietly between them.

Naming Emotions—and Learning Them Too

When Naomi turned three, she built a tall block tower all by herself. She beamed with pride—until the final block made it tumble. Pieces scattered. And she cried like her little world had fallen apart.

Harry, halfway through tidying up, started to say, "Naomi, it's not a big deal. Stop crying." But Florence gently touched his arm.

"Wait," she said softly. "Let's name it first."

Harry knelt beside Naomi. His voice was gentler this time.

"Are you feeling sad… or maybe frustrated because your tower fell?"

Naomi nodded, sniffled, and leaned into him.

Later that night, Harry admitted something.

"I didn't grow up like that. I didn't know you could name feelings. It's like I'm learning with her."

Florence smiled. "We both are."

A Lesson at Her Birthday Party

At Naomi's fourth birthday party, a cheerful uncle opened his arms wide and said, "Come here for a big hug, birthday girl!"

Naomi hesitated. Then she stepped back.

There was an awkward silence. A few relatives raised their eyebrows about it.

Florence gently placed a hand on Naomi's shoulder. "She doesn't feel like hugging right now," she said, calm and clear. "And that's okay."

Later that evening, when the house had quieted down, Harry sat with Naomi on the couch. "You did the right thing today," he told her. "Your body belongs to you. And if you don't feel like hugging someone, even if they're family—you can say no."

Naomi looked up at him, thoughtful, like something clicked.

That birthday, Naomi didn't just get a party. She got permission to have boundaries—and the assurance her parents would honor them.

Seeing Who She Is—Not Just What She Does

On a rainy Tuesday, Naomi came home from preschool with a crumpled drawing in hand—wild streaks of purple and green that spilled past the paper's edges.

Florence took the picture and studied it for a moment, then looked at her daughter with joy.

"I love how brave you were to try all those new colors!"

Harry smiled too. "You were kind to your friend today when she didn't have her lunchbox. That really shows your heart, Naomi. I'm really proud of you."

It wasn't about neatness or talent. It was about courage, kindness, and curiosity.

They weren't raising a performer. They were raising a whole person.

Grace When It Gets Messy

One rushed morning, the house was in chaos. Florence couldn't find her keys. Naomi's shoes were missing. They were late.

"Naomi, put your shoes on—now!" Harry snapped.

Naomi froze, lips trembling.

The guilt hit Harry immediately—but the moment moved on. Until bedtime, when he sat on the edge of her bed, looking down at her tiny face.

"I was wrong to shout," he said. "I was frustrated, but that wasn't your fault. I'm really sorry."

Naomi didn't say anything. She just reached out, wrapped her arms around his neck, and hugged him tight.

That hug? It was more than forgiveness. It was healing. For both of them.

Five Years In: What Had Taken Root

By the time Naomi turned five, she wasn't fearless—but she had faith.

She wasn't loud—but she was secure.

She wasn't always obedient—but she was learning to listen to her heart and to God.

Florence and Harry didn't follow a perfect plan.

They got tired. They messed up. They started again.

But they stayed present.

They prayed often.

They spoke gently.

They told the truth.

And they trusted that **God was parenting through them, not just beside them.**

That's what laid the foundation beneath Naomi's feet.

Reflection for Your Own Story

- When my daughter is upset, do I draw her in—or shut her down?

- What is she learning about God through the way I speak to her?

- Do I praise her character—or just her actions?

- Do I model grace and repair when I make mistakes?

Final Word: It's Not About Perfection

Florence and Harry didn't have all the answers.

They didn't have a parenting degree or a perfect game plan.

They just showed up—on the hard days, the happy days, and the in-between ones.

They gave Naomi presence. They gave her language. They gave her space to be her full self.

You can do the same.

Not perfectly.

But faithfully.

And in the small, quiet, everyday moments… **you'll be laying the foundation of a daughter who knows who she is—and whose she is.**

Chapter 2
The Early Years (Ages 5–7)

Growing Up, Growing Out: Guiding Your Daughter Through Exploration, Boundaries, and Friendships

"She's Growing So Fast... Am I Doing Enough?"

If you're anything like most parents, around this age, you start feeling that rush: your little girl isn't so little anymore. Suddenly she's chatting in full sentences, asking endless questions, and testing her independence like never before. One minute she wants your hand to hold; the next, she's insisting, "I can do it myself!"

It's a thrilling season — but also one filled with big questions and moments that can leave you wondering if you're getting it right. How do you balance freedom with guidance? How do you teach right from wrong without crushing her spirit? How do you prepare her heart and mind for the friendships and challenges ahead?

Why Ages 5 to 7 Are So Important

These years aren't just about learning the alphabet or how to count. They're about shaping who your daughter is becoming—her character, her confidence, her ability to understand and manage emotions, and the foundation of her faith and identity.

At this very age, she's soaking up *everything*—not just what you say, but *how* you say it as well. Your tone, your body language—your patience (or lack of it)—it all matters.

Here's the heart of it:

"These early years aren't about laying down the law, they're about laying down connection. When kids feel safe and loved, respect naturally follows."

For example:

Let's say your daughter spills juice on the floor. Again. You could snap, or you could kneel down, hand her a towel, and say, "Let's clean it up together nicely." One response teaches fear while the other teaches responsibility *and* relationship.

What's Happening Developmentally?

Social & Emotional Growth
By age 5 to 7, your daughter:

- Imitates friends' behavior and seeks their approval
- Begins to form deeper friendships with specific peers
- Understands and follows more complex rules
- Experiences bigger emotions and tries new ways to try and express them

What this means for you:
This is a time to gently guide, not shame. If she acts out something she saw at school or on TV, remember — she's exploring what it means to be social. Try something like:

"I noticed you said something unkind to your friend today. How do you think she felt? What can we do differently next time?"

Biblical reminder from Proverbs 15:1:

"A gentle answer turns away wrath."

Gentle correction plants seeds for a lifetime.

Language & Communication
Her sentences grow longer, her stories get more detailed, and her questions? Oh, the questions!

This is a perfect window to build emotional literacy by asking:

"Are you feeling angry, or maybe hurt?"

Teach safety basics too:
- "What's your full name?"
- "What's your address?"
- "Who's your mommy and daddy?"

These little phrases help her build awareness and safety.

Cognitive & Mental Development

She's learning:

- To count beyond 10
- To recognize letters and numbers
- To tell the major difference between what is real and what is a pretend
- Cause and effect

Imaginative play isn't just fun—it's also vital. When she plays "teacher" or "doctor," she's practicing empathy and creativity. Make effort to resist the urge to interrupt and say, "That's not real." Rather, allow her imagination to grow.

Physical Development

By this age, your daughter typically:

- Uses utensils well
- Toilets independently
- Runs, hops, skips, and might even try somersaults
- Dresses herself (though socks might be mismatched!)

Celebrate her body and growing coordination. Giving her small chores like watering plants or setting the table builds confidence and fine motor skills.

Common Challenges & How to Handle Them

Thumb-Sucking or Finger-Sucking
This soothing habit is common but can worry parents as permanent teeth come in. Don't force it; instead:

- Use positive reinforcement with sticker charts
- Understand triggers—often tiredness or anxiety
- Offer bedtime rituals like prayer and cuddles as replacements
- If needed, tools like thumb guards can help—always paired with emotional support

Bedwetting at Age 5
It's very normal for about 15% of kids at this age to wet the bed. Causes range from deep sleep to stress or physical readiness.

Avoid punishment. Instead:
- Limit liquids 1–2 hours before bed
- Encourage bathroom trips before sleep
- Create a calm bedtime routine without screens or sugar
- Celebrate dry nights on a calendar

Remember, grace over guilt is the goal. Just as God is patient with us, be patient with her.

Real-Life Story: A Dad's Quiet Faithfulness

Harry, a father in London, shared how his 4-year-old daughter Ava struggled with night fears and thumb-sucking. Instead of ignoring it, he used finger guard to help with the thumb sucking, he prayed for guidance and began reading Psalms with her every night. Slowly, the habit faded. Ava started saying, "Jesus is with me," before sleep.

The lesson? Consistency and connection always matter more than control.

Boundaries and Consent Basics

These early years are the perfect time to gently plant the seeds of body ownership and consent—lessons that will grow with her for life.

- Let her know it's okay to say **"no"** to hugs, kisses, or touches—even from people she loves. Her comfort matters.

- Remind her: **Her body belongs to her and to God.** It's a gift, and it's hers to care for and protect.

- Encourage her to speak up if anything—or anyone—makes her feel uneasy. You want her to know she can always come to you, no matter what.

These conversations don't have to be scary or heavy. They can be simple, everyday moments that build trust, confidence, and a deep sense of self-worth.

Try phrases like:

"Do you want a hug right now?"

"We always ask before touching someone."
"If something feels wrong, come to me. I will believe you."

This builds a very good foundation of trust and self-respect.

Friendship Navigation

Friendships become more meaningful—and sometimes tricky. Your daughter will face peer pressure, learn how to share, and deal with hurt feelings. Help her by:

- Listening without rushing to fix things
- Teaching kindness, empathy, and forgiveness
- Encouraging her to talk about her feelings openly

Remind her: real friends love you for who you are, not just what you do.

Milestone Summary (Ages 5–7)

Area	What to Expect
Social & Emotional	Imitates friends, seeks approval, forms friendships
Language	Speaks in full sentences, tells stories, asks questions
Cognitive	Counts beyond 10, recognizes letters, tells real vs pretend
Physical	Toilets independently, runs, hops, dresses herself

Final Thought: Formation Before Correction

It's easy to want immediate obedience. But these years are about *forming* her heart, not just correcting behavior. Ephesians 6:4 says:

"Do not exasperate your children; instead, bring them up in the training and instruction of the Lord."

Train with tenderness. Instruct with empathy. Lead with love.

Your daughter is growing, stretching, discovering who she really is. Let her *becoming* be shaped by connection—not control—and grounded in grace. The way you guide her now, with gentleness and understanding, lays the foundation for a lifelong relationship built on trust, respect, and love.

How One Family Did It #2: *Raising Naomi, Ages 5–7*

Growing Up, Growing Out — The Arthurs Navigate Curiosity, Friendships, and Foundations

Naomi was now six years old, and some days it felt like she was growing faster than what Florence could keep up with. Her questions came with surprising depth. Her opinions were strong. And her sense of independence? Let's just say, that there were battles over sock colors and bedtime stories.

"She's growing so fast," Florence said one night as she folded laundry. "I keep wondering—am I doing enough or are there still some more things to be done?"

Harry smiled without looking up. "We're doing our best. That's something."

Florence sighed. "Yeah, but what if we push too much and she loses her spark?"

Harry paused, thoughtful. "Then maybe we make sure she always knows we'll help her find it again."

Fairy Castles and Timers: Giving Freedom Within Boundaries

One rainy Saturday, Naomi transformed her bedroom into a fairy kingdom—blankets draped over her desk, plastic teacups laid out for stuffed animals, a tiara balanced slightly crooked on her head.

Florence poked her head in and asked, "May I help you decide where Princess Sparkle should sit?"

Naomi beamed. "Only if she gets the blue cushion. She's the queen of the clouds."

That afternoon, Naomi asked if her friend Mia could come over for fairy tea.

"Sure," Florence said. "Let's make a plan. You'll get 15 minutes just the two of you, and then I'll check in. Sound fair?"

Naomi nodded, already running off to prepare.

In that simple interaction, Florence learned the secret to this age: **Give space—but stay near.**

"Are You Lonely or Just Left Out?": Emotion Coaching in Real Time

The next week, Naomi came home from school quieter than usual. She sat at the kitchen table, poking at her apple slices.

Harry leaned over, gently. "Did something happen today that you would like to talk about to me now?"

Naomi's voice was small. "They didn't let me play."

He didn't rush in with a fix, or dismiss it. Instead, he asked, "Are you feeling lonely, or maybe a little left out?"

Naomi looked up, surprised. "Both."

They talked about what she could try next time—ways to ask to join in, or to play near the group until someone noticed. Before bed, they prayed together: a short, simple request for courage and new friends tomorrow.

It wasn't about solving everything. It was about letting Naomi know her feelings were safe with them.

"Trying Hard Is Bravery": Character Over Performance

After a tricky math worksheet one evening, Naomi threw her pencil down and buried her head under a pillow.

"I'm bad at this. It's too hard."

Florence sat beside her and rubbed her back. "Trying something hard? That's real bravery."

Harry added from the doorway, "You don't have to get it all right. God made you brave enough to try again."

Naomi peeked out. "Even if I mess up again tomorrow?"

"Especially then," Florence smiled.

Consent at the Barbecue

At a family barbecue, Naomi's great-uncle leaned in for a big kiss on the cheek.

Naomi gently stepped back and said, "No, thank you."

A few relatives looked uncomfortable. But Florence calmly placed a hand on Naomi's back and said, "It's okay. She doesn't want to be touched now."

Later that night, as Naomi curled her into bed, they prayed:

"God, thank You for Naomi's strong, good body. Help her keep listening to it, and honoring it."

No lectures. No shame. Just reinforcement of sacred boundaries.

Repairing What Breaks

One rushed school morning, everything was off. Naomi couldn't find her shoes, cereal spilled, and the clock was not their friend.

"Naomi!" Harry snapped. "We don't have time for this right now!"

She flinched. The car ride was quiet.

That evening, Harry found her doodling quietly and knelt down beside her.

"Hey. I was wrong to yell today. That wasn't fair. I'm sorry."

Naomi didn't say anything. But she wrapped her arms around his neck and held him tightly.

She was learning: **Love doesn't vanish when people mess up. It grows stronger when they repair.**

When It Didn't Go Well

Not every moment was a win.

One weekend, Florence filled the calendar: a playdate, a birthday party, music class, errands.

By mid-Sunday, Naomi was in tears. "I feel... squeezed."

Florence realized they hadn't given her space to just *be*. Her small voice had been crowded out by good intentions.

Another time, Naomi told Harry about a classmate who called her weird.

Instead of leaning in, he just brushed it off. "Don't be so dramatic."

Naomi then didn't bring it up again.

It wasn't that they were bad parents. It was just a reminder: **connection comes when you pause, not power through.**

Chapter 3
Developmental Milestones (Ages 6–10)

Growing Minds, Expanding Hearts, and the Sacred Mother-Daughter Bond

Between the ages of 6 and 10, your daughter is stepping into a bigger world—full of new friendships, fresh questions about what's right and wrong, and a deeper sense of who she's becoming. It's a beautiful, sometimes messy, time of rapid growth in her mind, heart, and spirit. And alongside all this change, the mother-daughter bond begins its own intricate dance—filled with love, tension, discovery, and healing.

What's Happening in These Years?

Cognitive Development

Her brain is working overtime:

- She's mastering complex thinking, solving problems, and figuring out how the world works.

- Cause and effect start to make real sense as she's connecting actions to outcomes in new ways.

- Her curiosity feels bottomless as she is asking "why" constantly—not just about facts but about people's feelings and choices.

- She's starting to understand fairness, justice, and even what it means to take responsibility for her actions.

How to nurture this:
Encourage her wonder, by asking questions:
- "What do you think might happen if...?"
- "How did that make you feel?"

These open-ended questions build her thinking and her empathy.

Emotional Growth
Between 6 and 10, her feelings grow richer and sometimes more intense:

- She's learning to manage frustration and disappointment, but she'll still need your gentle guidance.

- Friendships get more complicated—cliques form, and fitting in feels important, sometimes painfully so.

- Peer approval feels huge, and so does the fear of being left out or bullied.

This is where your steady presence matters most. Teach her to recognize bullying—not just the obvious, but the subtle kind like exclusion or mean words—and empower her to stand up or seek help.

Moral Development
Her sense of right and wrong sharpens:

- She wants to please adults but also tests boundaries to understand fairness.

- Empathy blossoms—she's starting to see the world through other people's eyes.

- Everyday choices like sharing, honesty, and kindness aren't just rules anymore; they're real challenges she faces.

Help her navigate these with stories, gentle questions, and your own example. Remind her: mistakes don't make her bad; they make her human.

Friendship Cliques, Social Confidence & Anti-Bullying
Friendships become more layered. Cliques can feel like a safe haven or a source of exclusion. Your daughter might struggle to fit in or feel pressure to conform. You can help her:

- Spot healthy friendships vs. toxic ones.

- Build resilience and confidence to be herself, even if that means standing apart.

- Practice kindness and inclusion, reaching out to those who feel left out.

If bullying happens—whether in person or online—listen without judgment. Take her seriously. Work with teachers or counselors if needed. And teach her this vital truth: bullying says more about the bully's pain than her worth.

The Mother-Daughter Bond: More Than DNA — A Dance of Love, Conflict, and Becoming

The mother-daughter bond is sacred but complicated. It's part mirror, part legacy, part unspoken language.

When the Mirror Feels Too Clear

Sometimes, your daughter reflects your own insecurities, mistakes, and struggles. That can hurt—it can make you want to fix her or rewrite her story to protect your own heart. But remember:

She is not your second chance. She is her own person.

Your role? Meet her where she is—with compassion, curiosity, and love. Let her become who she's meant to be, even when it's hard or unfamiliar.

When Connection Turns to Conflict

Clashes are normal, especially as she pushes toward independence. You want to keep her safe; she wants to explore on her own terms.

Her defiance isn't always about you. Her silence isn't rejection at all—it could be shame, confusion, or just needing space. Be her calm lighthouse in the storm.

Real-Life Story: Choosing Curiosity Over Control

Jennifer, a single mom, was locked in daily battles with her 15-year-old daughter Zoë—arguments about clothes, phones, slammed doors. One day, Jennifer asked:

"What do you wish I would do differently?"

Zoë's answer hit home:

"Stop trying to fix me all the time. Just listen."

Jennifer shifted gears, practiced patience, asked open questions instead of giving orders. Slowly, their relationship softened and Zoë began opening up again to her.

What Every Daughter Needs from Her Mother (Even When She Won't Say It)

- To be seen and accepted, flaws and all

- To know she won't be shamed for changing or making mistakes

- To feel safe sharing her messy, complicated feelings

- To trust your love is unconditional, not performance-based

- To see you living with joy and self-respect—not just sacrifice

Healing Your Inner Child While Raising One

Parenting your daughter can stir up old wounds—maybe your own mother was distant or critical. Maybe you swore you'd do better but find yourself repeating patterns.

Here's grace: you don't have to be perfect. Just stay aware and willing to grow. When you apologize for losing patience, admit you're still learning, and say "I love you" even when she's upset—you're breaking cycles and healing your family's story.

Ways to Deepen the Mother-Daughter Bond

Practice	Why It Works
Mother-Daughter Dates	One-on-one time builds connection without pressure
Write Notes or Letters	Words reach her even when she's not ready to talk
Share Your Stories	Shows her you were once a girl with struggles too
Let Her Teach You	Honors her growing independence and voice
Apologize First	Models humility and accountability without ego

Quick Exercise: The 3-Minute Mirror

Tonight, when it's quiet, stand before a mirror and ask yourself:

- What parts of my daughter reflect my younger self?

- Am I trying to "fix" her because I haven't forgiven those parts in me?

- What does she need from me that I didn't get?

Then write her a note—one sentence, one truth, one soft word. You don't have to give it to her. It's for your heart, a first step toward tender healing.

The mother-daughter bond doesn't have to be perfect. It just needs to be real. Tender. And willing to grow together.

How One Family Did It #3: Naomi's Middle Childhood (Ages 6–10)
Growing Minds, Expanding Hearts & the Sacred Mother–Daughter Bond

Naomi was six, then seven, venturing into school life with big questions and a growing soul. Her friendships became richer and more complicated. Her sense of fairness sharpened—and the mother–daughter bond shifted into something deeper.

Discovery, Grace & Connection: A Real-Life Moment

One afternoon, Naomi lined up her dolls on the living room floor and paused.

"Mom, why do some people get left out at school?"

Florence knelt beside her, meeting her question with another:

"What do you think leads to that?"

They talked about kindness, fairness, and God's heart for those who feel excluded. Naomi engaged with both head and heart—it wasn't just a rule to follow but a compassion to live out.

Navigating Friendship & Bullying (with Love and Strength)

A few weeks later, Naomi came home from lunch looking small.

"They wouldn't let me join their group today."

Harry pulled her gently into conversation.

"Did that feel like they weren't being fair? Or did it just hurt your feelings?"

Together, they role-played a response she could feel strong saying:

"That wasn't kind. Could we play together?"

They also made a simple plan together—trusted adults she can turn to, words to share, and a reminder:

She is not defined by exclusion, but by inclusion in love.

Celebrating Courage Over Correctness

When test day rolled around, Naomi came home looking disappointed.

"I made mistakes all over this math sheet."

Florence kneeled beside her chair and said softly,

"I noticed how hard you kept trying, even when it got tough. That's what matters."

Harry smiled from the doorway:

"That kind of courage matters to us—and to God."

They weren't focused on perfect answers—they were celebrating persistence and heart.

Deepening Their Bond Through Conversation

As Naomi edged toward her teen years, debates became very common.

"You're upset when I disagree with you, Mom, aren't you?"

Florence paused, took a breath, and said:

"Sometimes I am. But I want you to feel heard, not silenced. Can you help me understand what's behind your words?"

Over time, those conversations invited listening instead of blame. Naomi learned disagreement didn't mean rejection—it meant deeper connection.

A Cautionary Moment: When Curiosity Was Quelled

- **Curiosity dismissed**: When Naomi asked why God allowed pain, Florence said too quickly,

"That's complicated."

Naomi stopped asking. Her wonder went quiet.

- **Emotional shame**: Naomi shared she felt angry. Harry said,

"Don't be so dramatic."

Her emotional world shut down.

- **Performance pressure**: A focus on winning made Naomi equate love with achievement. Kindness, effort, and joy took a back seat.

Chapter 4
Cultivating Creativity (Ages 7–10)

Valuing the Journey, Not Just the Finish Line

*"For we are God's masterpiece. He has created us anew in Christ Jesus, so we can do the good things he planned for us long ago." — **Ephesians 2:10 (NLT)***

Your daughter is a unique masterpiece—created by God with a spark of creativity tucked inside her heart. Between ages 7 and 10, she starts to explore this spark in big ways. She's no longer just playing; she's is experimenting, imagining, and figuring out who she really is. Whether she's telling stories, building forts, painting, or dreaming up new inventions, this is a sacred time for her to stretch and grow.

But here's the thing many of us parents get tripped up on: we often focus too much on the *end product* — the neat drawing, the perfect performance, the winning project. Instead, what really matters is *how* she creates—her process, her effort, her joy, and her discoveries.

This chapter is your invitation to step back, walk alongside her with curiosity, and celebrate the messy, beautiful journey—not just the trophy at the end.

What's Happening in These Years?

Between 7 and 10, your daughter's brain and heart are expanding in amazing ways:

- **Thinking:** She's sharpening her ability to plan and focus, asking deeper questions about the world.
- **Friendships:** Connections grow more meaningful, but peer pressure starts to creep in.
- **Self-awareness:** She's noticing herself more—sometimes feeling self-conscious and eager to belong.
- **Morality:** She's seeing right and wrong through her own eyes and beginning to understand empathy.
- **Creativity:** Her imagination now mixes with real skills—writing stories, inventing games, building things.

She's not just copying anymore. She's asking herself:

"What do I love? What am I good at? What makes me come alive?"

1. Make Space for Creative Exploration

You don't need a very fanciful art studio or expensive instruments. Creativity thrives with freedom and simple tools:

- Crayons, paints, collage materials
- LEGOs, cardboard, tape
- Toy instruments or kitchen percussion
- Journals, story prompts
- Kitchen science experiments
- Books about animals, space, or other cultures

When family asks for gift ideas, encourage things that inspire curiosity and skill—not just distractions.

Remember: "Whatever you do, do it all for the glory of God." (1 Corinthians 10:31) Help her see creativity as a form of worship, not just performance.

2. Let Her Interests Be Truly Hers
Your daughter might surprise you! Creativity isn't always painting or music. It might be:

- Designing a board game
- Writing comics
- Coding a simple animation
- Cooking or sewing
- Building forts with rules

Don't narrow her world instead expand it. Let her explore whatever catches her heart.

3. Celebrate Effort, Not Perfection
Here's the golden rule:

The journey matters more than the result.
You've probably seen it happen:

- A child draws for hours but crumples the paper and that was because it's "not that perfect."

- A parent says, "That's nice, but maybe try this next time?"

- The child quits because she feels she's not good enough.

When we chase perfection, we steal the joy of creating. Instead, focus on her effort:
- "I love how you kept going even when it was tricky."
- "What was your favorite part of making this?"
- "You should feel proud of yourself."

These words teach her to love the process and build inner motivation.

> *"Do not despise these small beginnings, for the Lord rejoices to see the work begin."* — ***Zechariah 4:10 (NLT)***

4. When Failure Becomes a Teacher
Failure is part of growing. Let her spill the paint, break the LEGO tower, or forget her lines. Childhood is the safest place to fail — it teaches resilience without lasting harm.

Share your own very flubs and laughs:

"I once burned dinner, and we ate cereal instead—and laughed a lot."

Showing her that mistakes are normal and okay helps her bounce back with grace.

5. Real-Life Inspiration: Joanne and the Piano
Joanne had talent for piano but lost her joy under pressure from her aunt Allison, who wanted excellence all the time. Instead of pushing, Allison asked:

"Do you want to keep playing because you love it, or because I want you to?"

Joanne chose to stay—on her own terms. That shift made all the difference, turning piano into passion again. She learned that it's not about being perfect but about pursuing with heart.

6. Help Her Solve Problems
When she hits a roadblock of which she will, resist the urge to fix it for her. Try questions like:

- "What could you try next?"
- "What if you flipped it upside down?"
- " Will you want me to work on it with you for a few minutes?"

This builds her confidence, resourcefulness, and leadership skills.

7. Avoid Living Through Her Achievements
Your daughter isn't here to fulfill your dreams or fix old regrets. She's here to become the woman God designed her to be.

Pushing her to earn medals for your pride can:
- Crush her joy
- Fuel anxiety
- Mix up achievement with true worth

Encourage her to seek God's purpose, not human approval.

"Am I now seeking the approval of man, or of God?" — Galatians 1:10

8. Celebrate All Creative Expression
Show you value her creativity by:
- Displaying her art around the house
- Recording silly or serious performances
- Reading her stories aloud at dinner
- Sharing her projects with family and friends

Every small celebration says: *What you make matters.*

9. Spiritual Creativity: Reflecting the Creator
Remind her that creativity reflects God's nature. He is the original Creator, and she bears His image.

> *"In the beginning, God created..."* — **Genesis 1:1**

Encourage her to use her gifts to bring beauty, joy, and service into the world—just like God does.

10. Watch for Social Pressures and Emotional Hurdles
Around age 10, peer pressure, cliques, and self-consciousness start to challenge many girls. This can lead to gossip, exclusion, or even bullying.

Case in point: Mia and the Apology
When Mia was caught bullying a new girl, her mom Joanne addressed it directly—with consequences and conversation. Mia apologized, learned empathy, and grew from the experience.

Kindness and creativity go hand in hand. Your daughter's imaginative world must be rooted in empathy and respect.

A Final Word: Creativity Is a Lifeline
Creative girls:
- Face problems with courage
- Think outside the box
- Express emotions in healthy ways
- Bounce back from failure
- Know their worth comes from who they are, not what they do

You're not raising a robot—you're raising a whole, beautiful person with dreams, thoughts, and God's divine design.

Let her make messes. Let her change her mind. Let her build castles, write poems, and dance in socks on the hardwood floor.

Give her the freedom to explore—and the wisdom to grow.

> *"Let your light shine before others, that they may see your good deeds and glorify your Father in heaven."*
> **— Matthew 5:16**

She was made to shine.

How One Family Did It #4: Naomi's Tween Journey (Ages 10–13)

Growing Deeper Roots When the World Gets Bigger
As Naomi entered the preteen years, the world around her widened and life got more layered. Friendships shifted; questions about identity and faith deepened. Florence and Harry stepped into this season aware that Naomi needed freedom—and grounded boundaries more than ever.

Let's walk through a real slice of life—and see how the Arthur family navigated it with presence and grace.

Real Moment: The First Big Question
One evening around the kitchen table, Naomi set her fork down and shared:

"I don't feel like I fit in. Everyone seems to already know who they are. I feel behind."

Florence leaned in nicely with a tender heart, "What makes you say that?" she asked her gently.

Naomi paused. "I'm not sure who I am yet..."

Rather than rush to answer, Florence opened conversation after dinner, as husband Harry washed dishes.

"God made you—exactly as He planned," Florence said softly.

"Growing into who you're meant to be is a journey, not a competition."

Harry joined in. "No rush. We're discovering it with you."

Friendships: Love, Loss & Confidence
Soon after, Naomi returned from school distant and withdrawn.

Harry gently asked:

"Want to talk about what happened?"

Naomi said one friend drifted away, and others felt too middle-school-y.

Harry offered perspective. "Some friendships change. But true ones don't need masks."

He coached gentle words for Naomi to say:

"I value your friendship. Can we still hang even if things are changing?"

They also drafted a "trust circle"—adults at school or home she could talk to when she felt alone or confused.

Identity Through Service & Creativity
Naomi found herself drawn to music and environmental activism. At school, she helped start a recycling club—and at home, she experimented with song-writing:

Florence supported it all. She kept the creative corner from Naomi's younger years—and added a simple guitar nook and notebook for lyrics.

When Naomi wrote a song about belonging and hope, Harry asked:

"What's the message you want other people to hear?"

Naomi smiled, notes turned into a chorus—or a prayer.

Hard Conversations with Heart
When Naomi came to her parents with questions about girls at school making fun of her faith, Florence didn't respond with a lecture.

She asked,

"What meaning does your faith hold for you? What feels most meaningful—and what's hard?"

They talked through it—heard her fears, affirmed her belonging in Christ, and prayed for courage.

Chapter 5
Building Strong Relationships with Your Daughter

Nurturing Bonds That Shape Her Identity and Heart

The relationships your daughter has with you as both her mother and father—are like the roots of a tree. They do ground her, shape how she sees herself, and influence how she will grow to love and trust others. These connections are not just important; they're transformational.

But in today's world, many families navigate additional layers—cultural differences, racial identity, blended households, or co-parenting from different homes. These complexities are real, but they're also opportunities: opportunities to teach your daughter who she is, where she comes from, and how deeply loved she is—no matter the circumstances.

The Father-Daughter Relationship

More Than Shared Interests—It's Heart Work
Fathers often wrestle with how to connect with their daughters, especially as girls grow and their interests shift. But a gap in hobbies doesn't mean a gap in love or influence.

In fact, that gap is a chance to build connection through curiosity, empathy, and presence.

A strong father-daughter bond offers your daughter:
- A trustworthy male role model she can rely on
- A healthy understanding of respect and boundaries
- Confidence to face new challenges
- Emotional strength in social situations

Start Early, Stay Actively Involved
From her first breath, your presence matters. Being "hands-on" isn't just about helping with tasks—it's about showing up emotionally, consistently, and with intention. Little moments build very lasting trust.

Model Respect in Action
How you treat your partner teaches your daughter what she deserves in relationships. Kindness, patience, and respect at home become her blueprint for how she expects to be treated.

Break Stereotypes, Share Passions
No interest is off-limits. Whether it's sports, woodworking, coding, or gardening, invite her in. She learns she's capable of anything—and that gender doesn't limit her in anyway.

Peter and Emma's Story
Peter noticed his daughter Emma's fascination with space. Instead of dismissing it as a "boy thing," he joined her—reading books, visiting the planetarium, and stargazing. Their

shared wonder became a bridge of comfort and connection during school transitions.

Create Safe Spaces for Communication
Daughters often turn to their mothers for emotions, but fathers can be safe havens too. From ages 3 to 12, emotional openness is easier to nurture. Be the dad she knows she can talk to without judgment.

Teach Self-Protection with Love
Helping your daughter understand safety is about building her inner compass, not her fear. Teach her to say "no," recognize trustworthy adults, trust her instincts, and speak up when something feels wrong. Discuss consent clearly, so she knows her boundaries does matter.

The Mother-Daughter Relationship

Walking Together Through Growth and Change
Mothers and daughters often share a unique closeness, but it takes effort to nurture confidence and self-worth beyond appearances.

Celebrate Strength Beyond Looks
Girls hear too often that their value is in their beauty. Shift the focus to her kindness, courage, creativity, and determination.

Navigating Puberty and Body Image
Ages 9 to 12 bring new changes and questions. Honest, shame-free conversations about menstruation and growing bodies

are vital. Normalize these changes so she doesn't feel alone or embarrassed.

Francesca's Story
When Francesca started her period unexpectedly, she felt scared and ashamed. Her mother's gentle openness transformed that fear into understanding and trust. They shopped for supplies together so she could know how to do it, talked about what to expect, and Francesca felt empowered, not ashamed.

Normalize the Conversation for Everyone
Menstruation is a family matter. Including fathers in age-appropriate conversations helps remove shame and builds a culture of openness.

Model Positive Self-Talk
Your daughter is watching how you treat your own body. Avoid negative comments about food, weight, or appearance. Teach her that all bodies are worthy of love and respect—starting with her own.

Encourage Her Voice and Choices
Help your daughter speak up, even when it's really hard. Let her make decisions appropriate for her age. This builds independence and trust in herself.

Embracing Racial and Cultural Identity

Rooted and Proud in Her Story
Your daughter's racial and cultural identity is a vital part of who she is as well. Helping her embrace this fully builds resilience and confidence.

- Share stories of your heritage and family history—celebrate traditions, food, music, and language.

- Talk openly about race and difference, helping her understand and navigate the world with pride and wisdom.

- Affirm her beauty and worth in every aspect of her identity.

- Equip her to handle difficult questions or prejudice with grace and strength.

If you're raising her in a cross-cultural household, use the blend of cultures as a gift, not a challenge. Help her see herself as a bridge-builder—someone who carries multiple worlds in her heart.

Navigating Co-Parenting and Cross-Generational Families

Love and Stability Across Homes
When dad is absent or co-parenting across households, relationships can feel complicated. But love and connection don't have to be.

- Prioritize open communication between all caregivers.

- Keep your daughter's emotional well-being at the center, not adult conflicts.

- Establish consistent routines and values, so she feels secure no matter where she is.

- Use technology to bridge distances—video calls, shared calendars, and messages of love.

- Emphasize that she is loved fully by all the adults in her life, regardless of where she sleeps.

Grandparents, aunts, uncles, and close family friends can be part of her support network too. Multiple caring adults build a richer safety net.

The Heart of Strong Parent-Daughter Relationships

1. **Listening:** Give her your full attention. Hear her, even when it's hard or different from your view.

2. **Honesty:** Be very real about your feelings and encourage her to be real too.

3. **Trust:** Protect her confidence—don't share her secrets without her permission.

4. **Calm in Conflict:** When emotions flare, stay patient and steady. Remember, children often lash out because they're overwhelmed, not disrespectful.

5. **Boundaries:** Love and rules go hand in hand. Being a parent means holding firm with kindness.

6. **Availability:** Show up emotionally, even if only for a few minutes a day. Those moments add up.

7. **Quality Time:** Meaningful connection beats quantity. Put away distractions, and be truly present.

Final Thoughts

Your relationship with your daughter is the soil from which her confidence, joy, and identity grow. She might forget what you said—but she will never forget how you made her *feel*: safe, heard, valued, and unconditionally loved.

Parenting a daughter is a sacred journey—full of twists, surprises, challenges, and immeasurable rewards. Your daily choice to show up for her, in all her beautiful complexity, is the greatest gift you can give.

No matter your family's story—no matter the hurdles—your love, presence, and authenticity can be the anchor that helps her flourish.

How One Family Did It #5: Rooted in Relationship — Naomi Ages 9–12
"She Will Remember How You Made Her Feel"

It was 7:52 on a Wednesday morning when Florence caught herself—again—fussing over socks.

Naomi, now 10, was pulling on mismatched ankle pairs. One lime green. One a faded grey.

"They're just socks," Naomi said, shrugging as she reached for her bag.

Florence almost said something. About neatness. About presentation. About how the world can read a girl's shoes before they hear her voice.

But she didn't, she rather paused.

Maybe this wasn't about socks. Maybe it was about control. Or fear. Or trying to armor Naomi against a world that can be brutal and wasn't always kind to her.

So instead, she exhaled, sat on the edge of the bed, and gently asked:

"Are you okay today, baby?"

Naomi didn't flinch. She just looked up and whispered, "I'm tired. Of school. Of people. Of smiling when I don't feel like it."

Florence held out her hand.

"You want a hug or space?"

Naomi leaned in.

The Soil of Strong Relationships

Between ages 9 and 12, Naomi wasn't just growing taller—she was growing more complex. Friendships got deeper... and more confusing. School felt bigger. Her sense of identity stronger, but shakier too.

These were the years when Florence and Harry learned this wasn't the season for strict answers—it was the season for open hearts.

"She doesn't always need us to fix it," Harry told Florence once. "She needs to know we'll sit in it with her."

The Father–Daughter Thread: Tethering Trust

Harry and Naomi didn't share every interest. She was all about drama club and dream journals. He was all about barbecue recipes and fixing things around the house. Still, every Saturday morning, they took a walk together.

Sometimes they talked. Sometimes they didn't.

But it mattered.

When Naomi mentioned a boy in class who said her hair looked "weird," Harry didn't rush to fix it. He simply asked:

"Did it make you feel small?"

She nodded.

"You know who decides your beauty? You and God. That's it."

He didn't have to be a poet to be powerful.

What Harry Did:
- He asked curious questions, not leading ones.

- He listened more than he corrected.
- He showed up even when he didn't understand the whole story.

The Mother—Daughter Stretch: Closeness in Change

Florence and Naomi had once been in sync—same rhythms, same silliness. But now? Naomi could go quiet for a whole hour. Florence felt the gap growing—and feared it.

One day after school, Naomi slammed the door and disappeared into her room. No explanation.

An hour later, Florence tapped on the door with a bowl of strawberries.

"I'm not here to ask questions," she said. "Just here if you want company."

Naomi let her in. They sat on the floor in silence, eating slowly. It was awkward. But it was safe. And eventually—Naomi spoke.

That became their rhythm. Snacks and space. Silence and safety. Then, stories.

Rooting Naomi in Racial and Cultural Identity

When Naomi asked why a teacher always mispronounced her name—even after three years—Florence didn't brush it off.

"That's not small," she said. "Names matter. Yours has a rhythm and history that's sacred."

They practiced gentle correction together. They cooked jollof rice while listening to lively music. They told stories of grandmothers and villages and resilience.

Naomi wasn't confused about who she was. She was learning that identity isn't a burden—it's a birthright.

When Family Gets Complicated

Naomi had a half-brother from Harry's previous marriage. And sometimes, it was complicated.

Florence and Harry kept the communication clear and kind. They made space for Naomi to ask questions. And they kept reminding her:

"You're loved—fully, equally, always."

Naomi had a handwritten note in her journal from Harry that read:

You're my daughter by every measure that matters.

She folded it like a treasure.

Chapter 6
Ambition and Education

Raising Girls Who Believe in Their Brilliance—No Matter the Challenges

Every girl deserves to dream big and to believe she can achieve her goals. But ambition and education don't always come in that neat, predictable packages. For many girls—especially those with ADHD or learning differences—success requires more than just hard work; it requires understanding, support, and a little extra kindness toward themselves.

Raising Girls with ADHD

Seeing the Invisible Struggles

ADHD (Attention Deficit Hyperactivity Disorder) often looks different in girls than boys. While boys may show loud, energetic behaviors, girls' struggles often hide in quiet daydreams, forgetfulness, or emotional overwhelm. Because these signs are subtle, they're frequently missed—sometimes until middle school, or even adulthood.

A girl staring out the window might seem "shy" or "spacey," but inside, her brain could be racing, distracted, or overloaded. **Recognizing these early signs can make a big difference.** This will then mean that your daughter can get the deserved support she needs to thrive not just in school, but also in her friendships and emotional well-being.

Common Signs of ADHD in Girls
What to watch for:

- **Inattentiveness:** She might seem like she's daydreaming often, have trouble following instructions with multiple steps, misplace things, or come across as forgetful and disorganized.

- **Hyperactivity:** Restlessness, fidgeting, excessive talking, or high-energy activities that might be mistaken for being "just active"

- **Impulsivity:** Interrupting, blurting out answers, acting without thinking, or difficulty managing frustration

Remember: These behaviors don't mean your daughter is lazy or defiant—they're signs her brain works differently.

Supporting Girls with ADHD

From Diagnosis to Daily Support
1. **Seek a Professional Diagnosis:** A pediatrician or psychologist can help confirm ADHD, opening doors to targeted support.

2. **Create a Personalized Plan:** This might include behavioral therapy, academic accommodations like extra time or quiet testing spaces, executive function coaching, and sometimes medication.

3. **Partner with Schools:** Work with teachers and counselors to develop IEPs or 504 Plans that provide consistent support in the classroom.

4. **Celebrate Strengths:** Curiosity, creativity, empathy, and resilience are just a few of the unique gifts ADHD girls often bring.

Supporting Perfectionism and Anxiety

When High Standards Become a Heavy Burden

Many girls struggle with perfectionism. Many girls do wrestle with perfectionism, there is the pressure to get everything "just right." While striving for excellence can motivate, perfectionism can also quickly spiral anxiety, stress, and fear of failure.

Some signs to look out for:
- Constantly worrying about grades or needing others' approval
- Putting things off because they're afraid it won't be perfect
- Spending too much time on tasks—or not starting at all
- Having a hard time accepting or learning from mistakes

How to Help:
- Teach that mistakes are part of learning and growth—not signs of failure.

- Model self-compassion: Show your daughter how you handle your own imperfections with kindness.

- Encourage small, achievable goals instead of "all or nothing" thinking.

- Practice calming strategies together—deep breathing, journaling, or mindful breaks.

- Celebrate effort, progress, and courage to try—even when results aren't perfect.

Mental Health First Steps

Building Emotional Resilience Early
Mental health is as important as physical health. Helping your daughter understand and care for her emotional well-being sets a foundation for lifelong resilience.

What You Can Do:
- **Normalize feelings:** Emotions are part of being humans so she can know it's okay to feel sad, anxious, or overwhelmed sometimes.

- **Open Communication:** Create safe spaces where she can talk without fear of judgment or punishment.

- **Teach Self-Care:** Encourage activities that recharge her—whether it's art, nature walks, music, or quiet time.

- **Know When to Seek Help:** If anxiety or sadness feels overwhelming or persistent, reach out to a mental health professional. Early intervention makes a difference.

- **Empower Her with Tools:** Teach basic coping skills like naming emotions, problem-solving, and asking for help.

Building Early Academic Confidence

Every Step Forward is a Victory

For girls with learning differences or ADHD, school can feel like an uphill climb. Small wins—finishing an assignment, understanding a concept, speaking up in class—are huge achievements.

- Praise her effort, not just outcomes.
- Help her break tasks into manageable chunks.
- Create predictable routines and clear expectations.
- Celebrate unique ways she learns best—whether visually, through movement, or by talking it out.

Remember: Confidence grows when your daughter knows she's supported and capable—even on tough days.

Final Thoughts

Raising a girl with ADHD, learning differences, or anxiety means walking a path of patience, discovery, and unconditional love. It's about recognizing that her brain and heart may work differently—but that difference is not a deficit. It's a different way of being brilliant in a world that often doesn't fit every kind of mind.

With empathy, practical support, and belief in her, your daughter can not only manage her challenges—she can thrive because of them. Your steady presence and encouragement are the greatest tools she will ever need.

How One Family Did It #6: A Different Kind of Brilliance — Naomi, Ages 9–12
"She's Not Falling Behind—She's Finding Her Way"

Florence stood quietly outside Naomi's door. Inside, she could hear the sound of quiet sobs—muffled by the sleeves of a hoodie and frustration.

The math worksheet lay crumpled on the floor. Eraser bits dusted the carpet. Naomi's pencil had broken clean in two.

"I'm just... dumb," Naomi whispered to herself.

The words sliced through Florence like glass.

This wasn't about numbers anymore. This was about shame. About a bright, sensitive 10-year-old losing belief in her own mind.

Florence knocked gently.

"Hey, love. Want to take a break with me?"

Naomi sniffed.

"But I didn't even finish the first question."

Florence crossed the room and pulled her daughter close.

"It's okay. I don't care about that worksheet. I care about you."

And with those few words, Naomi exhaled—and melted into her mother's lap.

When Her Brain Worked Differently

Naomi had been diagnosed with ADHD six months earlier. But Florence had seen signs for years. The daydreaming. The tears after school. The missed instructions and half-packed backpack.

She wasn't "naughty." She wasn't "lazy."

Naomi was brilliant, but her brilliance didn't follow the usual rules.

Her brain wasn't broken—it was beautiful. But it needed scaffolding.

Florence and Harry had to trade old expectations for new tools.

"We stopped trying to force Naomi to work like everyone else," Harry said.

"We started learning how *she* works best."

What the Arthurs Did Differently

They didn't overhaul everything overnight—but they made small, intentional shifts.

Support Strategy What It Looked Like
Chunking Homework in 15-min blocks, with stretch breaks

Visual Reminders Sticky notes on the mirror, a checklist on the fridge

Positive Reinforcement A "Did It Anyway" jar—each note a celebration of brave effort

Quiet Study Spot Headphones, fidget toys, and a bean bag nearby

School Advocacy A tailored support plan with her teacher: movement breaks, extended time

And when things fell apart?

They didn't panic.

They paused. Took a breath. Started again.

Language That Reshaped the Atmosphere
Naomi struggled with perfectionism such that if she couldn't do something flawlessly, she didn't want to try.

So Florence started using phrases like:
- "Mistakes mean you're learning."
- "You're brave for starting, even if it's hard."
- "You're not a grade—you're a masterpiece."

They called them **truth anchors**—words Naomi could grab onto when everything else felt like it was sinking.

Caring for Mental Health as a Sacred Practice

Sometimes Naomi's anxiety spiked without warning. Especially when she was tired or overstimulated.

Florence learned to slow things down:

- They kept candles in the kitchen and calming playlists for late homework nights.
- They used lavender oil, hot cocoa, and soft pyjamas as their go-to reset tools.
- They journaled side-by-side—sometimes with words, sometimes with doodles.
- They saw a therapist when things felt big.

One night, Naomi whispered:

"Is it bad that I feel this much?"

Florence kissed her forehead.

"Not bad, baby. It means your heart is wide—and your mind is powerful. You're learning to steer it. That's what strength looks like."

What Thriving Looked Like in Their Home

Naomi wasn't collecting medals. But she was collecting courage.

Thriving, for her, meant:

- Turning in a project she started on her own

- Asking her teacher for extra time (without crying)
- Telling her parents when she needed a break
- Laughing after a hard morning
- Falling asleep knowing she was still loved—even on the messy days

Florence wrote the verse **Proverbs 31:25** on Naomi's bathroom mirror:

"She is clothed with strength and dignity; she can laugh at the days to come."

Because joy, even in the struggle, was still possible.

A Prayer Florence Whispered After Hard Days
"God, help me see my daughter not as a problem to fix—but a wonder to understand.

Give me gentleness when I feel stretched.

Remind me that her path is not slower—it's sacred.

May my love be a cushion, not a comparison.

And may she know, deep down: she is not behind—she is becoming."

Chapter 7:
The Internet and Media

Raising Girls in a Digital World—With Eyes Wide Open and Hearts Fully Anchored

Screens are everywhere. In our pockets, on our walls, in our cars, even in our children's backpacks. And while technology brings incredible benefits—education at our fingertips, connections across distance, a space to create and imagine—it also brings a unique set of challenges for today's girls.

Your daughter is growing up in a world where likes, follows, filters, and comments often speak louder than real-life voices. And in this fast-scrolling reality, the values we want to plant—self-worth, confidence, empathy, and discernment—can be easily crowded out by comparison, curated perfection, and invisible pressures.

This chapter is about helping your daughter stay grounded and wise in a digital world that rarely slows down.

Screens as the New "Comfort Tool"

It's easy to hand over a tablet when you need five minutes of quiet or peace—and in moderation, it's okay. But over time, screens can shift from helpful to harmful. When they become the default soother for boredom, emotion, or loneliness, girls begin to rely on digital stimulation instead of developing coping tools like creativity, conversation, or solitude.

Let's be honest: screens can become a parenting crutch, too. We've all had moments of exhaustion where technology feels like the only break we get. Grace for those moments. But also, wisdom to reset.

Social Media: A Funhouse Mirror

Even young girls—those not yet technically allowed on platforms like Instagram, TikTok, or Snapchat—are still influenced by them. They see videos through siblings, friends, ads, or YouTube. They absorb unspoken messages:

- "This is what pretty looks like."
- "This is what being popular means."
- "If you want attention, you need to act or look like this."

These messages shape how girls see themselves and others—especially in the **tween years** (ages 8–12), when identity and belonging become central.

Body Image and the Digital Mirror

Filtered selfies, "what I eat in a day" reels, before-and-after fitness clips—all create a silent culture of *body comparison*. And girls, even those who haven't hit puberty, begin to measure themselves by impossible and often edited standards.

Your daughter might not say, "I hate my body." But she might say:

- "Why don't I look like her?"
- "I want to lose weight."
- "She's so much prettier than me."

These are signals. Not failures. Not vanity. Just a reflection of a girl trying to understand herself in a world full of mirrors.

What You Can Do:
- Talk openly about how photos can be edited and filtered.
- Avoid complimenting only appearance—praise her effort, curiosity, kindness, and strength.
- Model self-acceptance. Speak kindly about your own body, especially around her.
- Watch content together. Pause and ask, "What do you think this is trying to make us feel or believe?"

Media Literacy: Teaching Her to See Beneath the Surface

Media literacy isn't just about blocking bad content—it's about **teaching discernment**.

Help her ask:

- "Is this real or edited?"
- "Is this trying to sell me something—or make me feel a certain way?"
- "How does this make me feel about myself?"

- "What would I say to a friend who felt the way I do after watching this?"

Empower her to think *critically*, not just consume passively.

The Culture of Comparison vs. The Culture of Caring

Social media often breeds a "compare and despair" mindset. But you can actively build a "compare and *care*" culture in your home.

Comparison says: *"She's better than me."*

Caring says: *"She's great, and so am I."*

Comparison says: *"I wish I looked like her."*

Caring says: *"Let me celebrate her and take care of me."*

This shift happens when we:
- Celebrate others without tearing ourselves down.
- Talk about emotions openly.
- Practice gratitude.
- Unplug regularly to reconnect with *real* life.

Setting Healthy Digital Boundaries

You don't need to be a tech expert to help your daughter form healthy online habits. You need to be very **consistent, compassionate, and connected**.

1. Involve Her in the Rules

Let her help create boundaries around screen time, platform use, and phone-free zones (like the dinner table or bedtime).

When rules are collaborative, they feel more like agreements than punishments.

2. Balance Tech with Real Life
Encourage time for reading, hobbies, chores, and outdoor play. The more full her offline life feels, the less she'll rely on the online world for identity or validation.

3. Use Tech as a Tool—Not a Crutch
Ask, "What are you using your screen for right now?" If the answer is mindless scrolling or emotional escape, gently guide her toward more life-giving options that is helpful.

4. Model What You Preach
Your daughter notices if your eyes are always on your phone. Be willing to unplug alongside her.

When It Gets Hard: Mental Health and Digital Triggers

If your daughter begins withdrawing, obsessing over likes, or showing signs of anxiety or body shame, don't panic—but do pay attention.

Signs to watch for:
- Frequent mood swings after being online
- Fear of missing out (FOMO)
- Negative self-talk ("I'm ugly," "No one likes me")
- Preoccupation with appearance, weight, or popularity

Start with a conversation: "I've noticed you seem down after going online—can we talk about it?"

Offer empathy first, advice second.

If needed, reach out to a counselor who understands tween or teen mental health in the digital age. Early support can prevent deeper struggles later.

A Real-Life Example: Sienna's Story

Sienna, age 10, loved watching fashion and makeup tutorials online. But slowly, she started obsessing over how she looked—comparing her features to influencers and worrying she "wasn't pretty enough." Her parents noticed she no longer wanted to take photos or be in group pictures.

Instead of banning screens, her mom invited her to talk. They watched a few videos together and talked about filters, camera tricks, and self-worth. Then they printed photos of real moments—camping, family birthdays, art projects—and hung them on her wall.

It reminded Sienna of who she was—*not just how she looked*. Slowly, her confidence started to return.

Final Word: Connection Over Control

You don't have to control every click. You just have to stay *connected*.

The internet will always evolve faster than we can keep up. But your daughter doesn't need perfection—she needs **a parent who walks with her**, asks good questions, sets loving boundaries, and helps her feel secure in both her online and offline identity.

Remind her often:
- She is more than a photo.
- She doesn't need the world's approval to be worthy.
- She was made for connection—not comparison.

With your steady hand and listening heart, she'll learn to navigate the digital world with wisdom, courage, and grace.

How One Family Did It #7: Through Her Eyes — Naomi, Ages 10–12

"Am I Pretty Enough?" — Navigating Media, Mirrors, and Meaning

It started slowly.

Naomi stopped wearing the glitter leggings she used to love. Her bedroom mirror—once covered in doodled sticky notes—became a place of long stares and quiet sighs. She began hovering near her parents' phones, asking about apps her friends used. And then one evening, she looked up from the couch and asked quietly:

"Mum… do you think I'm pretty?"

Florence turned, caught off guard.

"Of course I do, baby. But… why are you asking?"

Naomi hesitated.

"It's just… everyone online looks so perfect. And I don't. Not really."

Florence felt her heart sink.

It wasn't just a question. It was a cry for anchoring.

What Naomi Was Seeing (Even Without Her Own Account)
Naomi didn't have TikTok or Instagram. But she didn't need to.

At school, friends passed around videos and reels. She'd seen beauty tutorials, "before-and-after glow-ups," and kids rating each other's looks. She started asking about whitening strips, filters, and skincare routines—things no 11-year-old had ever cared about in their house before.

"It wasn't just curiosity," Harry said.

"It was comparison. It was pressure. It was quiet insecurity bubbling up."

What the Arthurs Did Next
Instead of shutting it all down, Florence took a different approach. She chose **conversation over control**.

They sat together and watched some of the content Naomi had seen.

"I didn't want to act shocked," Florence said. "I just wanted her to know she could talk to me about it."

She asked gentle questions:
- "Do you think this video is real or edited?"
- "What do you think this is trying to make us feel?"
- "Does watching this make you feel better—or smaller?"

And she told her what she most needed to hear:

"You are more than your face. More than your reflection. You are beautifully made—on purpose."

Healing the Mirror

One Sunday afternoon, Florence and Naomi printed out real photos:
- Naomi laughing with icing on her chin at her birthday
- Her hands covered in paint after an art project
- Her hair flying wild on a swing at the park

They taped them to Naomi's closet door.

"This is what beautiful looks like," Florence whispered.

"Joyful. Brave. Free."

Naomi smiled. It was small—but real.

Later that week, she asked if they could make a collage together. But not of influencers. Of women who inspired her—writers, scientists, poets, even Tabitha from the Bible.

They called it the **"Wall of Real."**

Boundaries They Built *With* Her
Instead of handing down screen rules, the Arthurs invited Naomi into the process.

Boundary	Why It Worked
No phones at dinner	Protected a space where everyone felt seen
Tech-free mornings	Gave Naomi a calm start without comparison
Watch content together	Turned screens into conversations, not silence
Ask "why" before watching	Helped Naomi notice how things affected her mood

"We want her to be aware, not afraid," Harry said. "And we want her voice in the process."

On the Harder Days
Sometimes, Naomi still came home downcast.

"Everyone's so pretty and confident," she'd mumble. "I just feel... invisible."

Florence never brushed it off.

She'd pull her close and say:

"You're not invisible. Not to me. And definitely not to God."

Sometimes they journaled side by side.

Sometimes they prayed over **Psalm 139**:

"I praise You because I am fearfully and wonderfully made."

And when the feelings grew bigger than they could hold alone, they called in a counselor—someone who could help Naomi sort through the static and find her voice again.

What They Said to Keep the Truth Close

When Naomi Said...	They Responded...
"I'm not pretty like them."	"Pretty isn't a contest. You are beautifully *you*."
"Everyone else has better hair/skin/clothes."	"Comparison steals your joy. Let's name what makes *you* shine."
"I wish I looked different."	"I hear you. But you were made on purpose—just like this."
"Why do I have to take a break from screens?"	"Because you deserve peace. Not pressure from a phone."

What They Reminded Her Spirit
- You are not your reflection.
- You are not your follower count.
- You are not a product to improve.
- You are a daughter of God—created, called, enough.

"Don't be concerned about outward beauty... let your beauty come from within." — *1 Peter 3:3–4*

What the Arthurs Want Other Parents to Know
You don't have to outsmart the algorithm.

You don't need to panic every time she sees something online.

You just need to **show up**—with steady love and a listening ear.

Because the world is loud. But your voice can be louder. Gentler. Wiser.

"One day," Florence said,

"I hope Naomi looks back and doesn't just remember what she saw in the mirror—but what she felt in our home:

Seen. Loved. Enough."

Chapter 8:
The Joy of Raising Daughters

Growing Together, Letting Go with Grace

Raising a daughter is one of life's greatest privileges—and one of its most humbling journeys. From her first steps to her first heartbreak, you walk beside her as her guide, protector, teacher, and biggest fan. But here's the quiet truth: while you're raising her, she's also shaping *you*.

She softens your edges. She challenges your assumptions. She teaches you, sometimes without even a word, how to be more patient, more present, more real.

Parenting a daughter isn't about perfection. It's about *relationship*—rooted in reflection, honesty, and the willingness to grow, together.

Authenticity Over Perfection

There's a common pressure parents feel: *Be strong. Hold it together. Get it right.* But the most powerful thing you can offer your daughter isn't perfection—it's *authenticity*.

Let her see your real self. The one who gets tired. The one who messes up. The one who apologizes.

Because when you show her that even grown-ups are still growing, you give her permission to be human too.

Let go of the myth that you must be always in control, always right, or always composed. Sometimes the strongest parenting moments come from soft places—when you sit beside her in silence, when you cry together, when you say, *"I don't have all the answers, but I'm here with you."*

Letting Go: Little by Little
One of the quiet heartbreaks of parenting is that it's a long, slow process of letting go.

You let go of her hand so she can walk.
You let go of control so she can choose.
You let go of the outcome so she can grow.

Letting go doesn't mean stepping back from love—it means stepping back from *control* and leaning into *trust*.

As your daughter grows, she'll face her own mistakes, disappointments, and risks. And even though everything in you wants to protect her, you'll find the greatest strength is in teaching her how to face life—not fix it for her.

Resilience: Building Strength Through Setbacks
Every girl will fall. Every girl will fail. Every girl will doubt herself.

That's part of becoming strong.

Our job isn't to remove her challenges—it's to walk her through them. To teach her that discomfort is not danger. That failure is not final. That pain is a teacher—not an enemy.

When your daughter faces rejection, setbacks, or self-doubt, stay close to offer empathy before advice. And remind her:

- "You are not alone."
- "You are capable of doing hard things."
- "This is one moment. It doesn't define your worth."

Help her see resilience not as bouncing back to who she was, but rising into who she's becoming.

The Power of Vulnerability

Take Julia's story. She had always been the "strong one"—never cried in front of her kids, never asked for help. But after losing her mother unexpectedly, Julia found herself crumbling. One day, while doing dishes, she broke down in front of her 11-year-old daughter, Ava.

Through tears, she said, *"I miss Grandma so much. And I'm trying really hard to stay strong, but some days are just hard."*

Ava wrapped her arms around her. In that moment, strength wasn't about holding it together—it was about letting her daughter see that emotions are nothing to fear and vulnerability became a bridge between them—not a burden.

Finding Joy in the Ordinary

The joy of raising daughters isn't just in the milestones—it's in the quiet rituals of everyday life.

It's in the messy art projects.
The awkward jokes at dinner.
The bedtime talks that turn into heart talks.

The mornings when you braid her hair while she tells you about a dream she had.

The music you deliberately dance to in the kitchen when nobody's watching.

Joy doesn't come from doing everything right. It comes from being fully *present*—from noticing the wonder in small, sacred moments.

Parenting Reflection: Growing Yourself, Too

Your daughter is watching you more closely than you think. Not for perfection—but for *integrity*.

Ask yourself often:

- Am I speaking to her the way I want her to speak to herself?

- Do I model how to ask for help?

- Do I show her that failure is part of life—not the end of the story?

- Am I letting go where I need to, and holding close where it counts?

Parenthood isn't static. It evolves—as we also do.

Final Thoughts: The Quiet Legacy of Love

When your daughter is grown, she may not or never remember every packed lunch or corrected homework. But she will remember how you made her feel:

- Safe, even in your imperfection
- Seen, even when she was struggling
- Loved, without condition or comparison

Raising daughters is an invitation to love fiercely, release gently, and reflect honestly. It's not about getting it right every time—it's about showing up, again and again, with your full, imperfect self.

And in doing so, you don't just raise a daughter.

You raise a woman.

You raise *yourself*.

How One Family Did It #8: The Joy of Raising Daughters — Growing Together, Letting Go with Grace

For Moms and Dads Ready to Embrace the Journey With A Heart, Honesty, and Hope

When their daughter Mia turned 11, Erin and Daniel Chen thought they were prepared. They'd read the books. Set the boundaries. Talked about "tween" stuff with knowing smiles.

But what no one quite prepared them for was how *quietly* the shift would happen.

One day, Mia still fit in Erin's lap, telling silly jokes. The next thing, she was closing her bedroom door more often, experimenting with eyeliner, and questioning *everything*—especially her parents.

"It felt like the ground kept moving under us," Erin said. "Just when we figured one stage out, she'd outgrow it."

But through the ups, downs, and deep sighs, the Chens began to realize:

They weren't just raising Mia.

She was raising them also, too.

Step 1: Choose Authenticity Over Perfection
At first, Erin tried to keep things polished—keep the house running, keep calm, keep smiling.

But after a long day and a missed work deadline, she broke down while loading the dishwasher. Tears slipped out before she could catch them.

Mia saw—and froze.

"Mom?" she whispered.

"I didn't know you got upset like that."

"I do," Erin said. "I just usually hide it. But maybe I shouldn't."

That moment unlocked something between them.

Vulnerability wasn't weakness—it was permission.

Try This:
- Let her see your humanity.
- Say, "I don't know, but I'm figuring it out too."
- Let go of the myth that strong parents never struggle.

"Be completely humble and gentle... bearing with one another in love." — **Ephesians 4:2**

Step 2: Letting Go, Little by Little

When Mia wanted to walk home from school with few of her friends, Daniel hesitated. He trusted her—but the world? Not always.

Still, he took a breath and said yes—with check-ins, of course.

"It felt scary," he admitted. "But I realized she needed those steps. And I needed to trust her."

The walk home became her space to laugh, talk, and learn to navigate her world.

Letting go isn't about pushing them away. It's about trusting that what you've planted will keep growing—even when you're not hovering.

Try This:
- Practice small acts of release.
- Support new experiences with gentle scaffolding.
- Pray together before big (and small) steps.

"Trust in the Lord... and lean not on your own understanding."
— **Proverbs 3:5**

Step 3: Build Resilience Through Setbacks

When Mia bombed a science quiz, she came home in tears, she was convinced that she wasn't smart enough.

Daniel sat beside her and said:

"You're allowed to be disappointed. But one grade doesn't get to tell your whole story."

They made brownies, reworked her study plan, and left the test behind.

Over time, Mia stopped spiraling every time things didn't go perfectly. She began to say, "It's okay—I'll try again and that was how she was helped."

What Helps:
- Validate feelings before offering solutions.
- Reflect on your own failures out loud.
- Celebrate progress, not just perfection.

Step 4: Be Real About Your Own Growth

There were days Erin snapped. Said the wrong thing. Got impatient.

But instead of brushing it off, she'd circle back.

"I shouldn't have yelled earlier. That wasn't about you—it was about me being stressed and I'm sorry about that."

Over time, Mia started apologizing too—not from shame, but from watching grace in action.

Questions the Chens Asked Themselves:
- Am I parenting from fear or trust?
- Do I model asking for help?
- What do I want her to believe about mistakes?

Step 5: Find Joy in the Ordinary
The Chens stopped waiting for the big moments to feel close.

They started baking on Tuesday nights. Dancing in the kitchen when dishes were done. Erin kept a shared journal where she and Mia wrote back and forth—sometimes silly, sometimes serious.

"I used to rush through almost everything that I did," Erin said.

"But when I slowed down deliberately, I realized these were the moments she'd remember most."

Try This:
- Make time for laughter—even on hard days.
- Let routine moments become sacred.
- Say yes to joy, even when life is messy.

Final Reflections: The Legacy You're Building
Mia's still growing. So are the Chens. And that's the point.

It's not about raising a daughter *perfectly*.

It's about being present, real, and willing to grow alongside her.

It's the quiet things she'll carry forward:
- The way you said sorry and meant it.
- The way you saw her when she didn't see herself.
- The way you stayed steady—even through your own storms.

What Mia Said One Night Before Bed

She was 12 now—too tall for Erin's lap, but not too old for bedtime chats.

As Erin kissed her forehead, Mia whispered:

"I like the fact that you don't try to be perfect, Mom. It makes me feel like I don't have to be either."

Erin smiled through tears.

"Good. Because you never had to be. You just have to be *you*."

Why This Chapter Works for Families
- Real stories from real parents walking the same road
- Scripture grounded in the day-to-day, not just the big moments
- Gentle truth for tired hearts
- Actionable ways to connect without adding pressure
- A reminder: parenting is soul-work, not performance

Chapter 9:
Body Image, Puberty & Identity

Growing into Herself with Grace, Truth & Strength

Puberty can feel like a minefield. Hair grows where it didn't before. Curves appear. Her voice changes. Her body sends signals — on schedule, early, or late. Meanwhile, the world around her — peers, screens, media — tells her she's never enough, never pretty enough, never small enough.

This very chapter invites you to walk very closely with your daughter through these changes—emotionally, spiritually, and physically—not with fear or shame, but rather with clarity, kindness, and conviction.

1. The Power of the Puberty Conversation

Scripture Reminder:
> "See, I have engraved you on the palms of my hands."
> **— Isaiah 49:16**

Even when changes feel overwhelming, God's design for her is not a mistake—it's intentional.

Real-Life Story: "When Sara's First Period Came"
Sara, a bright 11-year-old, got her first period unexpectedly at school. She panicked, felt ashamed, and told no one. By the time she texted her mother, she was in tears. Her mom drove to the school and reassured her: "This is something your body was made to do—and Grace (her sister) and I experienced it too." They laughed through tears. They went shopping together for her first pads. The talk wasn't about hiding but about understanding, dignity, and confidence.

How to Start the Conversation Before It Happens:
- Use casual moments: in the car, during bath time, after school: "Your body is starting to change—curves, hair—those are signs of health."

- Avoid shame language: call it **"becoming you"**, not "something your body has to handle."

- Normalize struggle: share your awkward moments. "I was terrified my first cycle. It felt like I was broken. Learning helped me feel strong instead."

2. Emotional & Spiritual Identity in a Changing Body

Puberty isn't just physical—it's spiritual and emotional.

Milestone Table: Ages 8–13

Age	Physical Signs	Emotional Themes	Faith Identity Tools
8–10	Notice breast buds, body hair begins	Embarrassment, curiosity	Introduce "My Body, God's Gift" Bible stories
10–12	Menstrual cycles start	Mood swings, insecurity	Scripture memory: *Psalm 139:14*, affirmation cards
12–13	More defined curves & hormones	Self-consciousness, comparison	Prayer journal: tracking gratitude + emotional notes

Practical Tool: The Identity Anchor Card

Create a laminated 4×6 card together with:

- Two truths (e.g. "I am loved by God. I am creative.")
- Two lies to fight ("I must be perfect. I am only my appearance.")
- A favorite Bible verse (e.g. *Psalm 139:14*)

Keep it in her school bag or mirror—something she can touch when doubt or comparison sneaks in.

3. Media Literacy & Healthy Comparison
Even more than before, social media becomes a highlight reel of other people's best selves—and young girls are watching.

Scripture Reminder:

> *"For am I now seeking the approval of man, or of God?"*
> *— Galatians 1:10*

Conversation Starters:
- Watch a typical Instagram reel together, pause it:

"What do you think she's really feeling?"

"Does her life look like yours? Is that okay?"

- Discuss how filters distort reality.
- Encourage "comparison breaking" statements:
- *"I don't need to look like her. I have gifts only I can give."*

Real-Life Story: "When Mia Unfollowed Influencers"
Mia, age 12, grew anxious comparing her body to influencers. Her mom helped her review her follow list. They decided together **unfollow** accounts that made her feel small and **follow** girls her age doing real things. Suddenly her feed showed more kids hiking, painting, reading—and she felt lighter.

4. Coping with Anxiety & Perfectionism in Puberty
Perfectionism and comparison often show up closely.

Red-Flags to Watch For:
- "I want to lose weight before school starts."
- "I messed up my hair, I'm too ugly to go."
- Excessive mirror checking or critical self-talk.

First-Aid Tools for Anxiety:
- **"Pause & Pray" Break**: breathe in for 4 seconds, out for 10, and pray, "God, help me know I'm enough."
- **"Kindness Counter"**: write one kind thing she did or said each day in a journal.
- **"Screen Detox Days"**: one day a week without any selfies/social media—replace with outside time or reading.

5. Building Worth Beyond Appearance

Your daughter's worth is never tied to her body. Help her anchor identity in soul, service, and spirit.

Story:
Grace had always been praised for being "pretty," but never celebrated for her kindness. Her mom shifted—saying, "That was so generous what you did for your friend." Over time, Grace began seeing that being caring mattered more than being cute.

Practical Tools:
- Praise non-appearance traits everyday ("I love how brave you were!")
- Volunteer or serve together—shift value from body to blessing.

- Create a "Strengths Jar"—fill it with slips written by family/friends that celebrate who she is inside.

6. Reflection Questions for Moms & Dads

- What stories about your growing body still echo in your mind?

- Do you model body kindness in what you say or do?

- Can you remember a time you felt worthy without being "liked"?

Write one small action you'll take this week to affirm your daughter's identity beyond image.

Final Thoughts: Who She's Becoming

Puberty is not just a season of physical transformation—it's a spiritual leap toward her unique God-given purpose. When you walk with her through the awkwardness, the discomfort, the comparison, and the change—not with shame, but with gentle truth—you plant seeds that grow into resilience, identity, and peace.

Your daughter is becoming. And who she becomes is far bigger than her body.

> *"You are fearfully and wonderfully made."* — **Psalm 139:14**

Hold that truth close. Whisper it over her. Let it light her way.

How One Family Did It #9: Growing Into Herself
A Family's Journey Through Body Image, Puberty & Identity

For Moms and Dads Ready to Walk Beside Their Daughter With Love, Faith, and Real Talk

When Nicole and David's daughter, Lila, turned 10, everything started shifting.

It was subtle at first—mood swings, longer showers, rolled eyes at bedtime prayers. Then came the tears over jeans that didn't fit, the offhand "I hate my thighs," and the dreaded, whispered question:

"Mom... am I fat?"

Nicole froze. She hadn't expected it this early.

"You're beautiful," she blurted out.

Lila shrugged. "You have to say that just because you're my mom."

And just like that, Nicole realized this wasn't about weight.

It was about *worth*.

And they needed to talk about it—now, not later.

Step 1: Start the Conversation Early—Open, Gentle, and Shame-Free

Lila got her period at school—panicked, bleeding through her jeans. The nurse called Nicole, who showed up in record time with a sweater and a quiet hug.

In the car, Nicole didn't lecture. She simply said, "This happened to me, too. I thought I was dying."

Lila blinked. "You were scared too?"

Nicole nodded. "Absolutely. But it wasn't scary forever. It became just another part of me."

They got some ice cream. Bought pads. Laughed a little. Cried a little.

And just like that, Lila knew: *this isn't shameful at all and I'm not alone in this.*

What You Can Do:
- Use car rides and bedtime to gently open the topic.
- Say things like, "Your body is changing, and that's a good thing. Let's talk about it."
- Share your awkward stories—she needs to know you were once unsure too.

"See, I have engraved you on the palms of my hands."
— Isaiah 49:16

Step 2: Help Her Anchor Her Identity — Spiritually and Emotionally

Nicole and Lila sat down one night and wrote two truths and two lies together.

Truths:
- "I am loved by God."
- "I am brave."

Lies:
- "I have to be perfect."
- "I'm only valuable if I'm pretty."

They called it Lila's *Anchor Card*—a little index card she kept in her backpack. Something to reach for when the voice of self-doubt grew loud.

It didn't erase every hard moment—but it gave her a lifeline.

Try This:
- Make an "Identity Card" with your daughter.

- Read Psalm 139:14 together and reflect: "What does this mean for me today?"

- Affirm who she *is*, not how she *looks*.

Step 3: Walk Through Media, Don't Just Monitor It

Lila didn't even have her own social media yet, but YouTube, iPads, and older cousins were enough. Suddenly, she was comparing herself to girls with perfect lighting, flawless skin, and filters no one talked about.

So Nicole and David started watching *with* her. Not to control, but to guide.

"What do you think this post is trying to say?"
"Do you feel better or worse after watching that?"
"What makes someone really worth following?"
They didn't demonize the internet.
They just taught her how to *discern it*.

Try This:
- Ask, "Does this content celebrate real life—or a fake version of it?"
- Introduce her to creators who talk about inner strength, creativity, or faith.
- Use Galatians 1:10 as a filter: *"Whose approval matters most?"*

Step 4: Address the Anxiety Hiding Beneath Body Talk

One day, Lila broke down in front of the mirror.

"My face is weird. My body looks wrong. Everyone else looks older. Better."

Nicole sat down on the floor beside her. She didn't try to fix it. She just said, "Tell me what you're feeling."

They started using a breathing rhythm together:

Inhale 4... exhale 10... then whisper, *"God, remind me I'm enough."*

Some days, they journaled. Others, they made silly videos or got hot chocolate.

But they always named the anxiety—and made sure Lila knew she was more than it.

What You Can Do:
- Watch for harsh self-talk, mirror checking, or food obsession.

- Replace "You're fine" with "That sounds heavy—let's sit with it together."
- Teach spiritual tools *and* seek counseling if needed.

Step 5: Build Worth That Outlasts the Mirror
Nicole started shifting how she complimented Lila.

Instead of "You look so cute," she'd say:

"I saw how patient you were with your brother today. That's beautiful."
"You stayed calm when you were frustrated—that's strength."

They also created a "Strength Jar"—dropping in notes each week celebrating character over appearance.

Lila started to glow from the inside out.

Not because she thought she was flawless—but because she knew she was *enough*.

> *"Charm is deceptive, and beauty is fleeting..."*
> **— Proverbs 31:30**

Step 6: Reflect on Your Own Story, Too
David realized he needed to be part of this conversation—not just Nicole.

So one night, he told Lila about his middle school acne and how he used to wear hats to cover his face.

"We all have things we'd change. But I want you to know: your value has *nothing* to do with how you look."

She smiled.

Parents, your daughter is watching how you treat *yourself*, too.

Ask Yourself:
- How do I talk about my own body?
- Do I criticize myself in front of her?
- Am I showing her what grace looks like when we mess up?
- Am I trusting God's design in my own life?

Final Encouragement for the Road Ahead

Puberty doesn't come with a manual—but it does come with **opportunity**.

To deepen connection.

To shape her understanding of identity.

To reflect God's love in the most ordinary, messy, sacred conversations.

Your daughter is not just changing—

She's becoming.
Becoming curious. Brave. A little unsure. Sometimes moody. Often brilliant.

She doesn't need perfection.

She needs presence. Yours.

Whisper truth into her fear.

Laugh when you can.

Pray when you're tired.

And keep showing up, over and over again.

Because long after she forgets the facts about hormones or hygiene,

she'll remember how you made her feel—

Seen. Safe. Loved. Enough.

Why This Chapter Connects
- Rooted in *real family stories* — not theories
- Offers *simple, practical steps* you can take this week
- Woven with *scripture and spiritual wisdom*
- Doesn't sugarcoat the awkward—meets it with compassion
- Designed to equip you emotionally, spiritually, and relationally

Chapter 10:
Friendships, Boundaries & Consent
Growing Connection, Confidence & Courage

The Importance of Healthy Friendships

Friendships between ages 6–12 are pivotal. They shape how your daughter sees herself, how she navigates social situations, and how she learns empathy, loyalty, and conflict resolution. Yet these relationships can bring joy—and also drama, exclusion, and peer pressure.

Teaching Personal Boundaries & Safe Touch

Your daughter's body is her own. Teaching her this truth—gently and clearly—is essential.

Practical Steps:

- Use proper names for body parts. Explain that private parts are private.

- Teach: *"You can say NO—even to family or friends—if it doesn't feel right."*

- Use scenarios that helps ("What if someone tried to hug you when you said no?") to practice her response.

- Make it very clear: *"No secret is a good secret. Tell me if someone asks you to keep a secret from mommy or daddy."*

Scripture Anchor:
"Above all else, guard your heart..." – Proverbs 4:23. Teaching self-respect puts protection in her hands—not fear in her heart.

Understanding Consent & Speaking Up
Consent isn't just physical—it's respectful communication.

- Explain consent in everyday terms: *"Permission before action."*

- Role-play: "If someone asks to borrow something, say 'Yes if you ask me first.'" or "If they don't ask, say, 'I'm not okay with that.'"

- Teach that feelings matter: "If it makes you uncomfortable, it's okay to speak up."

Weekly Tool:
Play **"Consent Check"**: while playing, pause and ask, "Are you okay with this?" Reinforce her right to decline.

Navigating Peer Pressure & Drama
Social dynamics shift very quickly in elementary and even in junior school. Cliques do form. Drama does stirs. It's a ripe season for comparison and even insecurity.

Empowering Strategies:

Situation	How to respond
Someone teases her about what she wears	*"I choose clothes that match who I am."*
A friend wants her to share a secret or exclude another girl	Teach her to say, *"That doesn't feel kind."*
She's pressured to do something risky (ruin homework, gossip)	Encourage: *"I'm not comfortable with that—it's not me."*

Real Story: Sarah and the Gossip Group

When Sarah's friends invited her to spread rumors about another girl, she felt torn. But she remembered a conversation with her mum— *"True friends lift, not laugh."* Sarah said, **"No thanks, that's not who I am."** She lost some friends—but gained respect and self-trust.

Cultivating Kind & Inclusive Friendships

Help your daughter:

- Befriend others who sit alone at lunch.
- Ask, *"Can I join in?"* instead of assuming exclusion.
- Lead rather than follow by initiating kindness.

Encourage gratitude: spotlight moments where she chose kindness over fitting in.

Social Comparison vs. Caring Culture

Social media or school gossip may lead your daughter to compare her body, clothes, or popularity.

Counter-Strategies:
- Teach **Media Literacy**: "Not everything we see is real. Many photos are filtered or staged."

- Practice affirmation: Every night, say: *"One thing I really loved about you today was..."* (e.g. generosity, humor, bravery.)

- Help her find friends and role models who celebrate differences—not replicate uniforms.

Scripture Anchor:
"For you formed my inward parts... I am fearfully and wonderfully made." – Psalm 139:13–14. God made her unique on purpose.

Boundaries with Tech & Social Media

As screen time grows, teach digital boundaries:

- No sharing passwords—only safe adults can see them.

- Ask: *"Would you say this in person? If not, don't say it online."*

- If she's uncomfortable or someone messages her inappropriately, she can show you—no blame, just love and help.

Practical Tools to Equip Her

1. **Role-Playing Kit:** Use dolls or action figures to act out scenarios—asking permission, standing up to bullying, saying no politely.

2. **Boundary Consent Chart:** Family puts sticky notes on this chart when someone respects a boundary—they get a smiley sticker.

3. **Safe Person Network:** Chart of 3–5 trusted adults she can go to with anything—no secrecy, no shame.

Final Hope Note

Your daughter is wired for connection, but she's not meant to lose herself to fit in. Teach her that kindness and courage often diverge from the crowd. Empower her to stand firm—not for popularity, but for peace, truth, and self-respect. You're not just teaching social skills—you're shaping inner strength.

May she grow into a woman who knows her worth, protects her body and heart, and loves others bravely.

How One Family Did It #10: Friendships, Boundaries & Consent

Growing Connection, Confidence & Courage

For Parents Helping Their Daughter Build Bonds — with Love, Protection, and Purpose

When Ella turned 9, her world got bigger—and messier.

One day she came home beaming, full of playground stories. The next, she shut her bedroom door and cried quietly into her pillow.

"Mom... I think I don't have any real friends."

Her mom, Kristen, wanted to fix it. But instead, she sat beside her on the carpet and said:

"Tell me what happened."

There was drama at recess. Someone got left out. Another girl made fun of Ella's white sneakers. It was that mix of hurt and confusion that's all too common in childhood friendships—where one minute you're best friends and the next you're invisible.

Kristen did realized something: this wasn't just about friendships. It was about voice. And boundaries. And self-worth.

And it was time to start *teaching*—gently, intentionally, and from the heart.

Step 1: Teaching Personal Boundaries & Safe Touch

When Ella's younger cousin tackled her in a bear hug, she stiffened. Her dad noticed and calmly asked:

"Ella, did that feel okay to you?"

She shook her head.

So he said to her cousin:

"Let's ask Ella first if she wants a hug."

No drama. Just respect.

They began using the correct names for body parts at home—no nicknames, no shame—and regularly said:

"No one has the right to touch your body without permission. Not even someone you know."

They also practiced role-playing simple moments:

- What do you say if someone hugs you and you don't want it?

- What if a friend wants to share a secret and says not to tell anyone?

Kristen reminded her:

"There's no such thing as a good secret that makes you feel bad."

Try This at Home:
- Use real names for body parts to build clarity and confidence.

- Encourage your daughter to ask *and* answer: "Is this okay with you?"

- Let her know: *Her no is enough.*

"Above all else, guard your heart..." — **Proverbs 4:23**

Step 2: Understanding Consent in Everyday Life
Consent isn't just about bodies—it's about respecting space, time, and feelings.

So Kristen and Ella made it very fun. They played the "Consent Check" game at home:
- "Can I play with your stuffy?"
- "Can I jump on the couch with you?"
- "Can I hug you goodnight or would you rather a fist bump?"

Ella started using consent language with friends too:

"Can I sit here?"
"Are you okay with that game?"

She was learning early that her comfort matters—and so does everyone else's.

Try This:
- Practice asking permission during regular moments.
- Praise her when she speaks up for herself—or checks in with others.
- Teach: "It's brave to ask. It's strong to say no."

Step 3: Navigating Peer Pressure & Playground Drama

Friendships got trickier around fourth grade. Ella came home upset after a group of girls laughed about another classmate's clothes.

She said, "They wanted me to join in... I didn't know what to do."

Kristen reminded her of a phrase they had practiced:

"That doesn't feel kind to me."

Ella didn't join the gossip. And though the girls pulled away, something surprising happened: a new friend noticed, and they started sitting together at lunch.

It was hard—but empowering.

What You Can Model:

Situation	What She Can Say
Teased about clothes	"I wear what feels like me."
Asked to exclude someone	"I don't like leaving people out."
Pushed to do something uncomfortable	"That's not for me. I'm good."

"True friends lift, not laugh." — A phrase they posted on the fridge

Step 4: Cultivating Kind & Inclusive Friendships
Kindness isn't just something to teach—it's something to celebrate.

At dinner, they had a new tradition: "Kindness Shoutouts."

Kristen would ask:

"Did you do something kind today—or notice someone else being kind?"

Ella shared moments like inviting someone to play or saying hi to the girl who often sat alone.

She started seeing kindness as something *active*, not passive. Something that is *brave*.

Ideas to Try:
- Encourage "invite-first" instead of "wait-to-be-asked."
- Praise courage when you see that she includes others or speaks up.
- Celebrate when she chooses compassion over coolness.

Step 5: Replacing Social Comparison with Caring
Ella wasn't online yet, but she'd already seen filters and influencers through friends' tablets.

One day, after looking at a cousin's TikTok, she asked:

"Why do I look different from all the pretty girls?"

Kristen's heart sank.

So they started naming the lies in media:

"That picture's filtered."
"Most people only post their happiest moments."
"Your worth isn't up for votes."

Every night, they added this to bedtime:

"One thing I loved about you today was…"

(Her creativity. Her laughter. Her courage.)

Bit by bit, Kristen watched her daughter learn:

I don't need to be like everyone else. I like who I'm becoming.

"I praise you because I am fearfully and wonderfully made."
— Psalm 139:14

Step 6: Creating Safe Digital Boundaries

Even before Ella had her own phone, they started building a "tech trust" mindset.

Their family rules were simple:

1. Keep passwords private—shared only with safe adults.
2. Ask before clicking. If it feels weird or icky, tell someone.
3. No shame if something confusing happens—just talk about it.

When a classmate sent an uncomfortable photo on a group text, Ella told Kristen immediately. There was no blame. Just love, protection, and next steps.

At Home, You Can:

- Role-play what to do if she sees something strange or mean online.

- Say: "You can always tell me. I'm not mad—I want to help you stay safe."

- Build a "Safe Circle" of trusted adults she can go to, anytime.

Practical Tools You Can Try

- **Friendship Role-Play** – Use dolls, animals, or LEGO figures to act out tricky scenarios: saying no, being left out, helping someone else feel welcome.

- **Consent & Respect Chart** – Add a sticker when someone in the family honors a boundary or checks in kindly.

- **Safe Person Network** – Make a card listing 3–5 adults she can talk to when something feels wrong or confusing.

Final Encouragement

Your daughter is made for friendship—real friendship.

Not the kind that demands she shrink, perform, or betray her values.

You are teaching her how to *see herself* clearly, so she can choose wisely.

You're showing her how to protect her heart without closing it off.

How to say yes to joy and no to pressure.

And above all:

You're raising a girl who knows she's worth standing up for.

Because you've shown her how.

Float these truths often:
- You don't have to fit in to belong.
- You don't have to be perfect to be loved.
- Your voice matters.
- Your heart is sacred.

When she walks into school, friendship, or life's future rooms, may she walk in whole, brave, and kind—because she's been taught that love and boundaries *can* go hand in hand.

And one day, when she comforts someone else, or speaks up, or steps away from what's not right, she'll carry your voice with her:

"You are strong. You are enough. And your heart is worth protecting."

Chapter 11:
Financial Independence & Purpose
*Raising Girls Who Know Their Worth
And How to Manage It*

Why Financial Confidence Matters Early

Teaching your daughter about money isn't just about dollars—it's about dignity. When a girl learns how to earn, save, give, and spend wisely, she builds self-respect and a sense of control over her future. Financial independence is a practical skill—but it's also deeply tied to purpose, confidence, and freedom.

Even in childhood, money can become a source of stress, entitlement, or insecurity. That's why it's very essential to start early—with age-appropriate tools that grow alongside her.

Ages 4–8: The Foundations of Value

Young children learn best through experience. Use everyday life to help her understand value, effort, and generosity.

Practical Tools:
- **Give her a small allowance** linked to tasks (like making her bed or helping set the table). Explain: "Money comes from effort."

- Use **three jars**: Spend / Save / Give. Let her decorate them and decide how to divide her money.

- **Talk about cost**: "This toy costs as much as five of your chores." Help her think in real terms.

Story: Mia and the Ice Cream Truck
When 6-year-old Mia wanted ice cream daily, her dad said, "You can use your own money." She paused. "Maybe I'll save for that sticker book instead." She began making choices—sometimes emotional, sometimes wise, but always growing.

Ages 9–12: Building Real-Life Habits
As your daughter matures, deepen the conversation. Let her earn through extra jobs that she do, track her savings, and understand what things really cost.

Ideas to Try Together:
- Open a **basic savings account** with her and review statements monthly.

- Show her the **family grocery budget**. Let her help plan a meal within $15.

- Set a **short-term goal** (like buying a toy or book) and help her plan toward it.

- Encourage **generosity**—give her a chance to donate to causes she cares about, even if it's just $2.

Scripture Anchor:
"Whoever can be trusted with very little can also be trusted with much." **—Luke 16:10**

Responsibility grows with practice—not pressure.

Future You: Planting Seeds of Purpose
Money is just a tool—but purpose is the compass. Show your daughter how financial confidence will help her to pursue dreams, support causes, and build a life that reflects her values.

Goal Setting Activities:
- Help her **visualize her future**: "What would you love to do when you grow up?" Talk through how money, time, and effort might play an role.

- Introduce the **idea of leadership**—not just being in charge, but serving others well, solving problems, and building a better world.

- Teach her about **women leaders** who started small: Mother Teresa, Priscilla Shirer, Corrie ten Boom and Christine Caine or your local community hero. Let her see what's possible.

Real Story: Leila's Lemonade Stand
When 10-year-old Leila wanted to raise money for an animal shelter, her parents helped her start a lemonade stand. She made signs, priced items, and learned to count change. At the end of the summer, she donated $58—and was hooked. "I felt powerful," she said. "Like I could do something real."

Conversations to Keep Having

Money and purpose aren't one-time talks—they're ongoing. Here are themes to revisit often:

- **Needs versus Wants:** "What do we need this week? What do we want?"

- **Delayed Gratification:** "Do you want to buy this right now, or can you wait?"

- **Being Generous :** "Who might need help right now?"

- **Personal Values:** "What really matters more to you, is it having lots of stuff, or making a difference while you can?"

Quick Tips for Parents

- Let her make *small mistakes* with money now. Better to overspend on candy at 10 than on credit cards at 20.

- Don't hide financial stress—explain it gently. *"We're not buying that right now because we're saving for something more important."*

- Avoid "money shame" or fear-based conversations. Frame money as a **tool for impact**, not just survival.

- Celebrate her efforts, not just outcomes: *"I saw how hard you worked to earn that!"*

Final Thoughts

Raising a daughter who is financially independent and purposeful doesn't mean turning her into a mini adult. It means giving her tools, space, and encouragement to understand her value—and how to live it out wisely.

The end goal isn't wealth. It's freedom. It's purpose. It's a life where your daughter feels confident to earn her own money, make meaningful choices, and pursue goals that light her up from the inside out.

And one day, when she's faced with a tough decision—about her career, her finances, or her future—she won't freeze. She'll remember what you taught her: *You are capable, you are wise, and you are worth investing in.*

How One Family Did It #11: Financial Independence & Purpose

Raising Girls Wo Know Their Worth — and How to Manage It

For Parents Who Want Their Daughter to Grow Wise, Generous, and Free

Dear Parent,

Let's be honest: talking to our kids about money can feel... awkward. Too "adult." Too complicated. Or maybe even too heavy if money's been a source of stress in your own story.

But here's the truth: money isn't just about math or bank accounts. For your daughter, it's about something deeper — *value*. Self-worth. Purpose. Wisdom. Freedom.

What she learns now — how to spend, save, give, and earn — will shape her future confidence far beyond the piggy bank.

This is the story of how one ordinary family started early, kept it simple, and raised a girl who didn't just *understand* money — she saw it as a tool to live with purpose.

Step 1: Starting Young — Teaching Value, Not Just Cost
Bible Anchor: *"Whoever can be trusted with little can also be trusted with much." —* ***Luke 16:10***

At age 6, Mia always wanted something: ice cream from the van, glitter pens, another unicorn keychain.

One day, her dad handed her three jars: **Spend**, **Save**, and **Give**.

He said, "These are your choices. You get to decide where your money goes."

When Mia realized that daily ice cream meant no sticker book later... she chose to wait.

That moment wasn't about ice cream. It was about learning she had power — and her choices mattered.

Try This at Home:
- Give a small, regular allowance (tied to simple tasks like feeding the dog or setting the table).

- Use 3 jars or envelopes she decorates herself.
- Celebrate thoughtful choices — especially when she chooses to *wait* or *give*.

What to Avoid:
- Giving money without explanation ("here, just take it").
- Shaming or guilt: "You always waste your money!"
- Instead, keep the tone light and empowering. You're planting seeds, not running a finance course.

Step 2: Ages 9–12 — Building Habits That Stick
As Mia got older, her parents upped the trust.

At 10, she opened a savings account with her mom. Each month, they sat down with cocoa and reviewed the balance.

Later, she helped meal plan a week with a £15 budget — including choosing ingredients for spaghetti and garlic bread. She beamed when the whole family liked her choices.

Why It Worked:
- Mia saw money as something *she could handle*, not something to fear.
- She got to *practice* — not just hear lectures.
- Her parents asked for her help — giving her a sense of real contribution.

Try This:
- Let her manage a small budget for a family meal.
- Support short-term savings goals (like a book or craft kit), helping her break it into steps.
- Encourage giving: "Is there a cause or person you'd like to support this month?"

Step 3: Connecting Money with Purpose

One Saturday, Mia read about a local animal shelter needing supplies.

She said, "What if I sold cookies and gave them the money?"

Her parents helped her set up a small stand with signs she designed herself. She raised £58 — and delivered it with her own handwritten card.

Later that night, she said, "I felt proud. Like I actually helped."

This Isn't Just Cute — It's Powerful.

She didn't just learn about profit. She learned about *impact*. And that's what girls need most — to know they *can* make a difference.

Try This:
- Ask: "What do you care about in the world?"
- Tie money to passion: saving for art supplies, a service project, or a dream trip.

- Share stories of women who steward money well — not just for gain, but for good (entrepreneurs, activists, missionaries, creators).

What Helped This Family Most
They leaned on tools like:

- **"A Smart Girl's Guide: Money"** – full of relatable quizzes and real talk

- **Spending Tracker Printables** – so Mia could *see* where her money went

- **Conversations, not lectures** – during walks, car rides, even dishwashing

They didn't aim for perfection. Just presence, consistency, and openness.

Conversations to Keep Having

Theme	Try Asking
Wants vs Needs	"Do we need it today — or just want it right now?"
Delayed Gratification	"Would you rather get something small now or save for something big later?"
Giving & Generosity	"Is there someone we could bless this month?"
Identity & Purpose	"What kind of woman do you want to be one day — and how might money help you live that out?"

Parental Reminders

- Let her *make small money mistakes*. It's better she overspends on a toy at 9 than overdrafts at 19.

- Be honest about your own learning curve. You're modeling humility and growth.

- Avoid money-shaming. Don't say: "We can't afford that!" Say: "We're choosing to spend our money differently this month."

- Celebrate the effort — not just the outcome.

Final Encouragement

You're not raising a financial expert.

You're raising a **wise, grounded, generous** girl who sees money for what it is: a tool, not a trophy. A way to build a life with purpose — not just a life with stuff.

When she someday earns her first paycheck, gives to someone in need, or says *no* to something that doesn't align with her values... she'll remember these early conversations. These jars. These moments at the grocery store or bank or kitchen table.

She'll remember **you**.

And she'll know:

She's capable.

She's trusted.

She's already enough.

Let money be one more way you raise her — not just to spend well...

but to **live well**.

Chapter 12:
Mental Health & Emotional Resilience

Raising Girls Who Know How to Feel—and How to Heal

Why This Chapter Matters

Mental health isn't a luxury—it's a foundation. Anxiety, perfectionism, low mood—these challenges don't just arrive in adolescence. Many girls begin noticing them between ages 8 and 12. When unaddressed, these feelings can grow roots that last a lifetime. Yet with awareness, tools, and compassion, your daughter can learn emotional resilience far earlier than you think.

Age 6–10: Early Signals and Strength-Building

Even younger girls can begin to show signs of pressure or emotional overwhelm. Their words—or silence—can tell us a lot.

Look for these early whispers:
- Worrying about mistakes or being perfect—even over small tasks.
- Avoiding difficult tasks for fear of failure.

- Saying things like, "I'm not good enough"—especially compared to friends or siblings.

Try This Evening Reflection:
At bedtime, ask: *"What made your heart feel heavy today?"* This simple question helps shift emotional burden into expression—and builds trust over time.

Scripture Anchor:
"Cast all your anxiety on him because he cares for you." —1 Peter 5:7
Teach her she can name her worry—and that she's never expected to carry it alone.

Ages 10–14: When Anxiety, Perfectionism & Sadness Surface

Tweens and early teens often begin to face new pressures—school performance, social belonging, and body image. Anxiety and perfectionism frequently arrive as twins—driven by fear of failure or judgment.

What this might look like:
- A girl who piles chores or homework on herself until she can't keep up.

- Someone who freezes during tests despite knowing answers.

- A daughter who compares her body, looks, or life to others constantly.

If left unchecked, these patterns can evolve into depression, persistent low self-esteem, or avoidance of challenges.

Emotional Tools Every Daughter Needs

1. Build a Rich Emotional Vocabulary
Help her go beyond "sad" or "mad"—teach emotions like *frustrated, disappointed, discouraged, guilty, overwhelmed*.

Use tools like emotion wheels or feelings charts, and practice labeling emotions out loud together.

2. Coping Strategies for Heavy Moments
- **Name it, don't shame it**: *"You feel anxious? That's okay—let's talk about why."*

- **Grounding exercises**: Describe five things you see, hear, feel—one breath at a time.

- **Movement breaks**: Walk, stretch, dance to reset her mind.

- **Creative breathing**: Imagine blowing up a balloon slowly with each inhale, releasing fear with each exhale.

3. Normalize Therapy & Help-Seeking
Make therapy as ordinary as going to the dentist: *"Talking with someone who listens can help you think clearly."* Praise courage for seeking help—not shame. If she sees you prioritize mental health—for her and yourself—it becomes a normal part of self-care.

Real Story: Maya's Perfection Paralysis

Maya, 12, was brilliant—but terrified of making mistakes. School projects stretched across weeks, but she'd wait until the last minute, frozen with anxiety. Then one evening, she missed a page of homework—she sobbed, pulling at her hair. Her mother gently said: *"Maya, you aren't your homework. You aren't how others expect you to be. You are mine and God's, and we love you always."*

With therapy and a new mindset—*"done is better than perfect"*—Maya learned to start early, ask for help, and breathe through fear.

Growing in Emotional & Spiritual Resilience

Scripture to Anchor Her Soul:
- *"God has not given us a spirit of fear, but of power, love, and a sound mind."* —2 Timothy 1:7

- *"Come to me, all you who are weary—and I will give you rest."* —Matthew 11:28

Practice memorizing and personalizing these verses together—add them to prayer, note cards, or bedtime chats.

Resilience Checklist: A Weekly Practice

Practice	Why It Helps
Emotion check-in (once a day)	Builds awareness and connection
Breathing + grounding exercise (daily)	Calms nervous system on demand
"Done better than perfect" challenge	Reframes progress over perfection
Therapy talk	Reduces shame, increases support-seeking
Scripture reminder	Roots resilience in spiritual truth

Exercise: Worry Jar & Truth Cards

- Let her write down worries on slips of paper, fold them into a jar. Once a week, empty the jar—talk through each worry gently.

- Create *Truth Cards*: short statements like *"I am loved," "I am enough," "God gives me strength."* Keep them where she can pull one when anxiety strikes.

Resources You Can Use

- Children's mood journals (e.g. HappySelf, Otis)
- Emotion wheels or posters for visual reference

- Local child therapists who specialize in girls and adolescents
- Simple apps for breathing exercises (e.g. Calm, Breathe2Relax)

Final Thoughts: Mental Health as Life Skill

Anxiety, pressure, sadness—they're not signs of failure. They're signals that your daughter is human—and that she might need support. By teaching her to name emotions, breathe through stormy moments, and seek help bravely—in counseling, prayer, or conversation—you're equipping her for life.

You're showing her: you can carry hard days. You can seek rest. And above all—you don't have to face worry alone. She'll learn that strength isn't the absence of struggle—it's walking through pain with support, honesty, and courage.

You are not just parenting her emotion. You're growing her resilience, soul by soul.

Chapter 13:
Raising Girls of Heritage/Cultural Identity

Honoring Her Story, Empowering Her Voice

> "For you are all children of God through faith in Christ Jesus. And all who have been united with Christ in baptism have put on Christ, like putting on new clothes... There is no longer Jew or Gentile, slave or free, male and female. For you are all one in Christ Jesus." **– Galatians 3:26–28 (NLT)**

Why This Chapter Matters

Raising girls from diverse backgrounds is a beautiful experience, powerful calling—and one that comes with unique challenges. Our daughters carry with them a legacy of strength, creativity, and resilience. They also carry the weight of bias, microaggressions, cultural misunderstanding, and pressure to conform.

Your daughter may be one of few—or one of many—in her school, neighborhood, or friend group who looks like her, speaks like her, or celebrates the traditions your family holds dear. Whether she's navigating racism or simply trying to "fit in," her identity is constantly shaped by how the world sees her—and how she learns to see herself.

This chapter is about helping her know she is more than enough.

What's Happening Developmentally?

Ages 6–12: Seeds of Identity, Awareness of Difference

Area	Milestones
Cognitive	Begins comparing self with others; noticing differences in skin tone, hair texture, accents, etc.
Social	Notices racial, ethnic, and cultural dynamics in peers and authority figures.
Emotional	Develops pride—or shame—in identity, based on family, media, and school environments.
Spiritual	Starts asking, "Where do I belong?" and "What did God make me for?"

1. Normalize Cultural Conversations Early

Silence around culture and race can feel like shame to a child. You don't need to make everything a lesson—but make it normal to talk about your history, your heritage, and the beauty of who she is.

- **Tell family stories**: "Your great-grandmother used to cook this every Sunday..."

- **Celebrate holidays that reflect your culture**.
- **Talk openly about racism**: "Sometimes people judge based on skin, not character. That's wrong—but we stand for truth and love."

Try This:
"Have you ever felt left out because of your name, your hair, or your family's traditions?"

Listen. Validate. Don't dismiss.

2. Teach Her to Recognize Microaggressions

Many girls from diverse backgrounds will encounter subtle racism before overt discrimination. It might sound like:

- "You're pretty—for a Black girl."
- "You don't act Asian."
- "What are you? Where are you really from?"

Help her name these experiences, and guide her toward responses that are firm but kind.

You're equipping her to protect her peace without compromising her dignity.

"Be strong and courageous. Do not be afraid... for the Lord your God goes with you." – Deuteronomy 31:6

3. Speak Purpose Over Her Identity

Remind her that she was created with intention and beauty, not in spite of her background, but through it. Her skin, her language, her story—all of them are all sacred.

Speak these truths often, they do help:
- "You were born with a purpose."
- "Your voice matters."
- "Your history is power, not shame."
- "God delights in every shade and story."

Psalm 139:14: *"I praise You because I am fearfully and wonderfully made; Your works are wonderful, I know that full well."*

4. Bridge Faith and Culture

Don't make her choose between her culture and her spirituality. Instead, help her see how the two can inform and elevate each other.

Show her that:

- Her prayers can include her mother tongue, if she knows it.

- Her worship can reflect her cultural rhythms.

- Her hairstyle, clothing, and heritage are all expressions of divine creativity that is unique.

Real Story:
Zara, age 11, once said, "I felt like God didn't love people who looked like me—because none of the Bible characters I learned about did."

Her mother began reading Bible stories from children's books with diverse illustrations and shared African and Middle Eastern Christian heroes. Zara lit up.

Representation is not about ego—it's about *belonging*.

5. Equip Her to Navigate Peer Pressure & Fitting In
Your daughter may feel pressure to:
- Straighten her hair to match classmates
- Change her name to something "easier"
- Avoid speaking her family's language in public

Instead of shaming her for these instincts, ask:
- "What makes you feel that way?"
- "What do you think it means to be accepted?"
- "What does God say about fitting in?"

Then, remind her: She is allowed to code-switch. She is allowed to be both—faithful and fashionable, proud and private, confident and still learning.

Tool: Identity Wall
Have your daughter create a collage with images, words, and colors that reflect her own identity. Hang it where she sees it daily. Let it evolve as she grows.

6. Include Extended Family and Community
Family plays a very powerful role in shaping cultural pride. Involve grandparents, aunties, church leaders, and mentors who reflect your daughter's heritage.

Attend community events.

Read books with diverse authors.

Listen to her stories—and share yours.

"Tell me something you love about where we come from."

"Who's a woman in our culture you admire?"

Let her learn that she's not just one little girl—she's part of something *much bigger*.

7. Resilience Through Faith
Teach her that her worth is *not* dependent on being accepted by the world. It's already established by God.

When she faces exclusion, ignorance, or racism, equip her with:

- Scripture to lean on
- Safe adults to talk to
- Language to advocate for herself

Romans 12:2: *"Do not conform to the pattern of this world, but be transformed by the renewing of your mind."*

Final Word: She Is Not Alone
Raising a girl from a diverse background is not just about protecting her—it's about preparing her.

It's about rooting her in her story while giving her wings to soar.

It's about helping her hear God's voice above the noise of the world.

It's about showing her that being different is not a deficit—it's a *divine design*.

Your daughter is history in motion. She is legacy in the making. She is exactly who she was created to be.

*"Let your roots grow down into Him, and let your lives be built on Him." – **Colossians 2:7***

How One Family Did It #13

Raising a Girl from a Diverse Cultural Background
Honoring Her Story, Empowering Her Voice

When Nina was six, she came home from school very quiet. Too quiet. Her usual storytelling-about-everything energy had dimmed.

Her mom, Asha, gently asked, "Did anything happen today, sweetheart?"

Nina paused, fiddled with her sleeve, then mumbled, "A girl said my lunch was weird. That it smelled funny. And she said my hair was poofy."

Asha took a breath—deep and slow. She could feel her chest tighten. She remembered feeling the exact same sting when she was Nina's age. And now, here it was again, in her daughter's voice.

But Asha also remembered something else: how she *wished* someone had told her, back then, that her difference wasn't something to hide—but something to treasure.

So that night, they cooked the same dish—*chickpea curry*—together.

As the spices filled the kitchen, Asha said, "You know, your great-grandma used to make this every Sunday. She never wrote the recipe down. She said you have to *feel* when the spices are right."

Nina smiled. "So I'm part of her too?"

"Yes," Asha nodded. "You carry her in your hands. In your heart. Even in your cooking."

That weekend, Asha helped Nina create a little poster for her room—**"I'm Proud of My Story."** It had pictures of her family, her favorite traditional outfit, the food she loved, and a drawing of her curly hair in bold, joyful swirls.

They called it her "identity wall." It was her reminder: *I belong. I matter. I carry something beautiful.*

The School Incident
A few weeks later, Nina came home a little stronger.

"A boy asked if I was from somewhere else... like not from *here*," she said.

"What did you say?" Asha asked.

"I said, 'I was born here. And my family comes from somewhere really cool. Want to see the food my grandma taught me to cook?'"

Asha smiled. "And?"

"He said yes! He liked it. He even said it smelled *awesome*."

Wrestling with Identity
But the journey wasn't all smooth.

At age 10, Nina asked if she could start straightening her hair—"Just to try," she said.

Asha didn't scold her at all. Instead, she asked, "Why, love?"

Nina hesitated at first. "It's just that ... most of the girls at school have straight hair and mine gets all frizzy. I just want to fit in."

Asha gently replied, "I understand wanting to blend in with them. I really do. But baby, your hair grows the way God designed it—free, strong, bold. You don't have to change it to belong."

They sat down and looked through pictures of women—writers, scientists, athletes—who wore their curls and their heritage with pride.

Then Asha said, "You can choose how you wear your hair. Just make sure it's out of love for yourself—not fear of others."

Church and Culture

In their faith community, Asha noticed Nina sometimes felt unsure—like her culture wasn't reflected in the songs, the sermons, the stories.

So they started doing small things at home:

- Reading Bible stories featuring people from diverse backgrounds.

- Praying in Asha's first language once a week.

- Playing worship songs that felt familiar to Nina's ears and rhythms.

Slowly, Nina began to see that God wasn't far from her heritage—He was right in it. Her skin, her name, her story... were sacred.

Building Confidence Through Her Village
Asha also made sure Nina had mirrors—strong, joyful, loving women in her life who reflected back her worth.

She took Nina to heritage festivals. They read books by diverse authors. They invited Grandma to tell bedtime stories about when she was a girl in another country, making her way in a new world.

And when Nina turned 12, they added one more thing to her "identity wall"—a verse:

"I praise You because I am fearfully and wonderfully made."
— Psalm 139:14

The Last Conversation (So Far)
One night, just before sleep, Nina whispered:

"Mom... sometimes I still wish I didn't have to explain who I am to.... I wish people just *knew with much explanation* ."

Asha tucked her in and said:

"I know, my love. But explaining doesn't mean proving. You don't have to prove your worth to anyone. Your roots run deep. You're standing on something strong."

And Nina smiled, because for once, that truth felt a little more real.

Final Reflection

This is how one family did it.
They didn't have all the answers.

But they chose to talk, not silence.

To celebrate, not just protect.

To build identity not from the outside in—but from the inside out.

They raised a girl who knew that her story was her strength.

And that difference is not a burden—but a beautiful, divine design.

Please leave a 1-click Review!

I would be incredibly thankful if you can take just 60 seconds to write a brief review on the platform of purchase, even if it's just a few sentences!

Conclusion
The Journey of Raising a Girl With Purpose

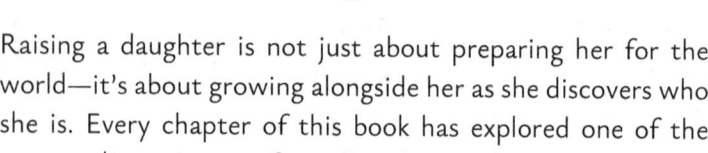

Raising a daughter is not just about preparing her for the world—it's about growing alongside her as she discovers who she is. Every chapter of this book has explored one of the many dimensions of girlhood: confidence, identity, friendship, mental health, culture, purpose. And underneath all of it is one essential theme: **growth**.

A **growth mindset** in parenting doesn't mean getting it right all the time. It means staying teachable. It means asking hard questions of yourself before placing hard expectations on your daughter. It means recognizing that parenting is not about perfection—it's about presence.

You Are Her First Teacher

From her earliest days, your daughter watches how you speak, how you respond to stress, how you treat others, and how you treat yourself. She learns what it means to be kind, to set boundaries, to recover from failure—not by your words alone, but by your example.

So when she makes a mistake, ask yourself:

Am I modeling grace?

When she's upset, ask:

Am I responding with empathy—or reacting with control?

When she questions her worth, ask:

Have I been reminding her of how deeply she is loved—by me and by God?

Your behavior teaches far more than your rules ever will.

The Power of Showing Up

There will be moments when you're tired, confused, or unsure if anything you're doing is "working." That's normal. You are not alone.

But showing up—again and again, with love, honesty, and intentionality—is what matters most. Your daughter doesn't need a flawless parent. She needs a **safe one**. One who listens. One who grows. One who apologizes when they get it wrong and tries again with love.

Even when she pushes back. Even when she's quiet. Even when she says she doesn't need you—**keep showing up**.

What This Book Fills That Others Miss

So much parenting advice focuses on behavior management. But this book dares to go deeper—to the heart of parenting girls in a changing world:

- We explored emotional intelligence, not just obedience.

- We honored cultural identity and intersectionality.

- We addressed mental health, faith, purpose, and media literacy as central—not optional—parts of parenting.

- We didn't shy away from hard conversations, because your daughter won't shy away from them either.

Where other books might give tips and tricks, this book offers tools and truth.

Keep Going: The Teenage Years Are Next

If your daughter is nearing adolescence, this is not the end—it's the beginning of a new chapter.

To continue building on what you've started, I invite you to explore the companion titles:

Parenting Teenage Girls and Raising teenagers wisely.

These books do dive deeper into the challenges of puberty, identity shifts, digital pressures, dating, academic stress, and more. They're grounded in faith, empathy, and the belief that teenage girls need guidance—not control.

One Final Word of Encouragement

Every time you listen instead of lecture, affirm instead of assume, and grow instead of guilt—you are planting seeds.

Seeds of confidence. Seeds of purpose. Seeds of emotional safety.

And one day, those seeds will bloom into a woman who knows who she is, who trusts her voice, and who walks into the world with courage, clarity, and compassion.

Because of you.

So thank you—for doing the deep work, for staying in the conversation, and for choosing presence over perfection. The legacy you're building isn't just for your daughter. It's for the daughters who come after her, too.

You are doing holy work. Don't underestimate it.

Other Books You'll Love!

1. The Fear of The Lord: How God's Honour Guarantees Your Peace

2. Parenting Teenage Girls for Purpose: Guiding Godly Young Girls to Walk in Charisma, Character, Calling, Life Skills, and Christ-Centered Confidence

3. Parenting Teenage Boys for Purpose: Guiding Godly Young Girls to Walk in Charisma, Character, Calling, Life Skills, and Christ-Centered Confidence

4. Raising Teenagers to Choose Wisely: Keeping your Teen Secure in a Big World

5. Spelling one: An Interactive Vocabulary & Spelling Workbook for 5-Year-Olds. *(With Audiobook Lessons)*

6. Spelling Two: An Interactive Vocabulary & Spelling Workbook for 6-Year-Olds. *(With Audiobook Lessons)*

7. Spelling Three: An Interactive Vocabulary & Spelling Workbook for 7-Year-Olds. *(With Audiobook Lessons)*

8. Spelling Four: An Interactive Vocabulary & Spelling Workbook for 8-Year-Olds. *(With Audiobook Lessons)*

9. Spelling Five: An Interactive Vocabulary & Spelling Workbook for 9-Year-Olds. *(With Audiobook Lessons)*

10. Spelling Six: An Interactive Vocabulary & Spelling Workbook for 10 & 11 Years Old. *(With Audiobook Lessons)*

11. Spelling Seven: An Interactive Vocabulary & Spelling Workbook for 12-14 Years-Old. *(With Audiobook Lessons)*

12. Raising Boys in Today's Digital World: Proven Positive Parenting Tips for Raising Respectful, Successful, and Confident Boys

13. Raising Girls in Today's Digital World: Proven Positive Parenting Tips for Raising Respectful, Successful, and Confident Girls

14. Raising Kids in Today's Digital World: Proven Positive Parenting Tips for Raising Respectful, Successful, and Confident Kids

15. The Child Development and Positive Parenting Master Class 2-in-1 Bundle: Proven Methods for Raising Well-Behaved and Intelligent Children, with Accelerated Learning Methods

16. Parenting Teens in Today's Challenging World 2-in-1 Bundle: Proven Methods for Improving Teenager's Behaviour with Positive Parenting and Family Communication

17. Life Strategies for Teenagers: Positive Parenting, Tips and Understanding Teens for Better Communication and a Happy Family

18. Parenting Teen Girls in Today's Challenging World: Proven Methods for Improving Teenager's Behaviour with Whole Brain Training

19. Parenting Teen Boys in Today's Challenging World: Proven Methods for Improving Teenager's Behaviour with Whole Brain Training

20. 101 Tips For Helping With Your Child's Learning: Proven Strategies for Accelerated Learning and Raising Smart Children Using Positive Parenting Skills

21. 101 Tips for Child Development: Proven Methods for Raising Children and Improving Kids Behavior with Whole Brain Training

22. Financial Tips to Help Kids: Proven Methods for Teaching Kids Money Management and Financial Responsibility

23. Healthy Habits for Kids: Positive Parenting Tips for Fun Kids Exercises, Healthy Snacks, and Improved Kids Nutrition

24. Mini Habits for Happy Kids: Proven Parenting Tips for Positive Discipline and Improving Kids' Behavior

25. Good Habits for Healthy Kids 2-in-1 Combo Pack: Proven Positive Parenting Tips for Improving Kid's Fitness and Children's Behavior

26. T Raising Teenagers to Choose Wisely: Keeping your Teen Secure in a Big World

27. Tips for #CollegeLife: Powerful College Advice for Excelling as a College Freshman

28. The Career Success Formula: Proven Career Development Advice and Finding Rewarding Employment for Young Adults and College Graduates

29. The Motivated Young Adult's Guide to Career Success and Adulthood: Proven Tips for Becoming a Mature Adult, Starting a Rewarding Career, and Finding Life Balance

30. Bedtime Stories for Kids: Short Funny Stories and poems Collection for Children and Toddlers

31. Guide for Boarding School Life

Your Free Gift!

As a way of saying thank you for Your purchase, I have included a gift that you can download at TCEC publishing .com

References

[1] https://cchp.ucsf.edu/sites/g/files/tkssra181/f/SelfEsteem_en0710.pdf
[2] https://www.theseus.fi/bitstream/handle/10024/50239/Anttila_Marianna_Saikkonen_Pinja.pdf
[3] https://ijcat.com/archives/volume5/issue2/ijcatr05021006.pdf
[4] https://www.harvey.k-state.edu/family-and-consumer-sciences/family_and_child_development/documents/CommunicatingwTeenTrust.pdf
[5] https://www.researchgate.net/publication/283721084_Early_Reading_Development
[6] https://www.understood.org/en/friends-feelings/empowering-your-child/building-on-strengths/download-hands-on-activity-to-identify-your-childs-strengths
[7] https://www.wfm.noaa.gov/pdfs/ParentingYourTeen_Handout1.pdf
[8] https://www.helpguide.org/articles/depression/parents-guide-to-teen-depression.htm?pdf=13027
[9] https://www2.ed.gov/parents/academic/help/adolescence/adolescence.pdf
[10] http://centerforchildwelfare.org/kb/prprouthome/Helping%20Your%20Children%20Navigate%20Their%20Teenage%20Years.pdf
[11] https://www.childrensmn.org/images/family_resource_pdf/027121.pdf
[12] https://educationnorthwest.org/sites/default/files/developing-empathy-in-children-and-youth.pdf

www.ingramcontent.com/pod-product-compliance
Lightning Source LLC
Chambersburg PA
CBHW050235120526
44590CB00016B/2096